How To Invest In Self-Storage

Scott Duffy
RK Kliebenstein

MiniCo, Inc.

Published by MiniCo, Inc., Phoenix, Arizona

ISBN 0-9771578-0-6

Cover Design by George Bernal

*T*ABLE OF CONTENTS

CONTENTS

OREWORD

Of all the misconceptions about self-storage, the one that amuses me most is the idea that self-storage is boring. *You rent a space, stuff in your stuff and drive away... how interesting could this be?* On the contrary, storing is not boring! The business operations of the self-storage industry are endlessly engaging. In fact, over its almost 40 year history, self-storage has been in a near-constant state of transformation, proving to be one of the most dynamic, powerful and vital business concepts in the world today.

Would it be possible to encapsulate the entirety of the self-storage enterprise into a guide-book that would be practical for even the newest newcomer? The short answer is "yes and they have." The long answer lies deeper in this book. When Scott Duffy and RK Kliebenstein first shared with me the idea and theme of their new project—a "how-to" book for self-storage—we were certainly intrigued. RK is well known in the self-storage industry and to me personally. He gained many years of experience as a self-storage executive, developer and investor before turning his attention to consulting. He is in high demand as a speaker and individuals both within and outside the industry seek his counsel about the business of self-storage. By contrast, Scott is relatively new to the self-storage industry. However, his knowledge, skills and experience in the business world have made him a welcome addition. I expect that he will continue to infuse the self-storage industry with his brand of thoughtful enthusiasm and innovative entrepreneurial spirit. I knew the challenge to create this book was great, but had no doubt these two gentlemen were up to the task they had set for themselves. Now, we suggest that *How To Invest In Self-Storage* offers value and benefits for existing self-storage professionals, as well as those investigating the industry and it's potential, perhaps for the first time.

How To Invest In Self-Storage is a tidy package of self-storage information, advice, examples, recommendations and fair warnings that we believe will be extremely useful to anyone who is seriously considering a future in self-storage. The customer base for self-storage facilities is remarkably diverse, and it's one of the reasons that the self-storage industry has continued its growth and profitability. Change of almost any kind may create an opportunity for self-storage utilization. It's not surprising then that self-storage, as an industry, attracts a similarly diverse audience of people interested in investment opportunities for development, operations and self-storage ownership.

One of the key issues our industry faces today is market saturation: too much self-storage product available in a specific geographic area. The authors make the point early in this book that the "if you build it, they will come" mentality can be a recipe for disaster for any new investor and poses a significant threat to other existing facilities in any particular market. The guidelines and oversight offered by Messrs. Duffy and Kliebenstein represent a sound approach to making an educated entry into the wide world of self-storage.

As with any endeavor, what you put into it will have a decisive effect on what you get out of it, and the authors make the point clearly and often that successfully investing in self-storage requires advice, knowledge, skill, effort and patience. This book offers a sound beginners' course in the lessons of self-storage and will certainly be an asset to those individuals with the drive and dedication to invest and enter this complex and evolving industry.

I am a self-storage optimist!   I believe that opportunity for continued self-storage growth still exists in most U.S. markets. Further, I applaud those professionals who have helped to steer self-storage through its start-up, growing pains and the success we know today. And for you, the reader, I am optimistic as well. Heed the advice spelled in these pages, do the work, believe in the possibilities, and you may indeed find the right "space" for your self-storage goals.

Hardy Good
Chairman & CEO
MiniCo, Inc.

PREFACE

I never thought that I'd write this book.

But one day I woke up and, probably like many of you, I realized that I was tired of getting up early and working hard all day for a paycheck. I was tired of giving up my evenings and weekends because of work. I was tired of spending more and more of my "free" time away from family and friends.

I needed to make a change.

What I wanted was more control over my life. What I needed was a vehicle that would provide me with the freedom, flexibility, and financial security I had always wanted. The problem was I had no idea where to find it.

For the next year I went on a mission. My objective was to identify the best business or investment opportunity that was available to help me achieve my goals. During that time, I read everything I could get my hands on and met with several people who were already living the life I wanted.

The advice that I got from these mentors was clear and consistent. They all insisted that the best way for me to take control of my life was to spend my time building *high cash flow, low maintenance* businesses capable of generating *passive income*. With this in mind I searched for business and investment opportunities that fit this profile. The more I searched, the more I realized how difficult this type of opportunity is to find.

The funny thing about life is that sometimes the best ideas come to us at the most unexpected times and from the most unexpected places. That's what happened to me. That's how I found self-storage, or better yet, how the self-storage business found me.

You see, the older I got, the more "stuff" seemed to accumulate in my house. I didn't actually need all the things that were piling up, but for some reason I couldn't let go. Then one day, I simply ran out of space. I needed a place to store my things.

Like many, I had never rented a self-storage unit. I had heard stories about old run-down facilities located on the edge of town. The images I had about storage made me very apprehensive about renting a space. I had visions of walking into an old, dingy, poorly-lit building with little to no security. This was hardly the kind of place where I wanted to keep my things.

Nevertheless, I canvassed the area where I lived. Then one day on my way home from work, I decided to stop into a self-storage facility. I had no idea what awaited me.

The whole experience was nothing like I expected. First of all, the location was convenient.

I passed it on my way to and from work every day. Second, the facility was safe. High-tech security systems including perimeter fencing, electronic gates, a password-protected entrance and exit, closed circuit video cameras, and individual door alarms on every storage unit made this facility seem as secure as a fortress. It was certainly more secure than any place I had ever lived. Third, the facility itself looked and felt much like a five-star hotel. Fourth, the customer service was outstanding and equivalent to the best retail and service businesses I had visited.

In short, this was a place where I *wanted* to keep my things!

The more I walked around, the more intrigued I became with the entire operation. I learned from the manager that almost every unit was rented and that there was a waiting list for several unit sizes. Rents per square foot were equal if not higher than nearby industrial, commercial, retail businesses, and even some local apartments. Maintenance costs appeared to be low. Best of all, the business was scalable. Like the parking lot business, it didn't seem to matter whether you had one space or 1,000 spaces. You still needed only one person collecting the tickets or running the front desk.

Determined to learn everything I could about this industry, I embarked on a crash course in self-storage. I soon discovered that the self-storage business was relatively unsophisticated and highly fragmented. There were very few sources of information, and I had a long list of questions, but finding the answers was not easy.

Over time, my perseverance began to yield dividends. I began by partnering with the most successful leaders in the industry. I tracked down the most successful companies, broke down how they achieved their results, and modeled their approach to quality and profitability.

Like any education, mine took patience and lots of hard work. At times, I was forced to learn through trial and error. I also suffered several setbacks. Luckily, none of those prevented me from moving forward and continuing on my path.

In the end, my biggest breakthroughs came from aligning myself with the right people, most notably RK Kliebenstein. With his help, I put together a great team and a detailed plan. I learned that, done correctly, self-storage can be a very successful, high cash flow, low-maintenance business. I also learned that when approached incorrectly, a self-storage business can turn into a disaster.

Now, RK and I have written this book in the hope that readers will uncover this unique investment opportunity for themselves. In the pages that follow, you'll discover the reasons and solid financial principles that make self-storage such a great business investment.
In putting this book together, we've compiled information from the best of the best in the self-storage industry. We've broken this information down into basic, easy-to-use ideas that will help you get the most out of your self-storage business. As you learn from our experience, you'll begin to decipher the language of self-storage. You'll learn how to get where you want to be financially, and we'll show you how to identify and take advantage of the best opportunities in self-storage.

Whether you're interested in investing in self-storage or want advice on running an existing facility, this book is the perfect place to start. RK and I firmly believe that our fast-growing industry has only just left the starting blocks. This book will point you toward the finish line so that you too can profit from self-storage in the years ahead. Join us now and take your first steps toward self-storage wealth, security, and the wonderful freedoms they bestow.

—Scott Duffy

ACKNOWLEDGEMENTS

I began this project over a year ago with no clear understanding of how much time and effort would be involved. This book would never have been completed without the unwavering support of my family and friends. I am indebted to these individuals who volunteered their time and expertise and provided critical guidance every step of the way.

I want to thank my family in particular for their love, encouragement, and support. I'd also like to thank those who took a chance on me, as well as those who served as mentors along the way. I would especially like to thank Don Sinclair, Kenny Baines, Mark Moses, Tony Robbins, Mike Hutchison, David Hutchison, Tom McCarthy, Chris Cottle, Jed Savage, Chris Kitze, and Ross Levinsohn.

I would also like to thank my co-author, RK Kliebenstein. Those of you who are just discovering the self-storage industry will soon get used to hearing RK's name. He is a pioneer, whose many years of dedication and hard work have helped self-storage achieve its modern status as one of today's best investment opportunities.

—SCOTT DUFFY

The training and experience I have contributed to this writing is a blessing from God. He has faithfully entrusted me with the stewardship of knowledge and placed many people in my path who have enriched my life, both professionally and personally, enabling me to share and communicate what I have learned. Of the most influence have been Dr. Kenneth Woolley and Neal Seeley, who have contributed greatly to the shaping of my career.

I am forever indebted to my co-author, friend and colleague, Scott Duffy, for without him, this would never have come to fruition. Without the constant support of my wife, Lorraine, I would not have the passion to pursue my professional endeavors and I thank God most for her love and patience.

I want to thank the countless other professionals in the self-storage industry who have contributed many thoughts and ideas that have been developed in this book.

—RK KLIEBENSTEIN

SPECIAL THANKS

We would like to acknowledge all those in the self-storage industry who helped to shape this project and provided valuable feedback. Special thanks go out to:
- Hardy Good, Chairman & CEO, MiniCo, Inc.
- Denise Nunez, President, Publishing, MiniCo, Inc.

- Marilyn Leslie, President, Asian Operations, MiniCo, Inc.
- Ed Olson, Principal, A-American Self Storage
- Craig Olson, Principal, A-American Self Storage
- Jim Davies, Principal, Buchanan Storage Capital
- Eric Snyder, Principal, Buchanan Storage Capital
- Ray Touhey, Principal, TNT Property Management
- Dianne Tanna, Principal, TNT Property Management
- Bruce Jordan, Principal, Jordan Architects
- Glenn Fuller, Self Storage Council, Norman, Cormany, Hair, & Compton
- Carl Touhy, Principal, Bancap Real Estate
- Marc Boorstein, Principal, MJ Partners
- Kenneth Woolley, Chairman & CEO, Extra Space Storage
- Terry Bagley, President & CEO, Centershift
- Bill Hobin, Principal, William Warren Group
- Troy Bix, Group Publisher, Virgo Publishing and *Inside Self Storage Magazine*
- Teri Lanza, Editorial Director, *Inside Self Storage Magazine*
- Charles "Chico" LeClaire, Marcus & Millichap
- Steve Osgood, CFO, The Amsdell Companies (U-Store-It)
- Harvey Lenkin, CEO, Public Storage Inc.
- Chuck Barbo, CEO, Shurgard Storage Centers
- Mike Burnham, CEO, StorageMart
- Mike Mikkelson, CEO, Liberty Investment Properties
- Hugh Horne, Director, Extra Space Storage, Inc.
- Ray Wilson, Principal, Self Storage Data Services
- Brent Wessell, SVP, GE Capital
- Steve Hryszko, VP Acquisitions, Amsdell Companies (U-Store-It)
- Aaron Swerdlin, First Vice President, CB Richard Ellis Self Storage Advisory Group
- Bob Benner, Principal, Bob Benner Real Estate
- Greg Wells, Grubb & Ellis
- Bruce Manley, CEO, United Stor All Centers
- Jeff Anderson, CEO, Stor-All Systems
- Carol Shipley, President, United Stor All Centers
- Don Murney, President, Don Murney & Partners (Former CFO U-Haul)
- Anne Ballard, Principal, Universal Management
- Michael Scanlon, President, Self Storage Association
- Chris Sonne, Principal, Self Storage Economics

Finally, none of this would have been possible without our meticulous editor, Daniel W. Gilbertson. A master at his craft, Daniel took an idea and made it into a reality.

ABOUT THE AUTHORS

Scott Duffy is an entrepreneur and investor whose instinct, talent, and dedication led him to become a self-made millionaire before the age of 30. He is the Founder and President of Self Storage Capital Group™, a Los Angeles, Calif.-based real estate investment company that specializes in developing, acquiring, and managing public self-storage facilities.

Prior to his self-storage ventures, Scott was a key member of several high profile media and technology companies. His resume includes names like Fox Sports, CBS Sportsline, and NBC Internet. Scott began his career working with best-selling author and speaker Anthony Robbins.

Scott, who makes his home in Los Angeles, California, has overcome several personal and professional challenges on his way to becoming a recognized leader for innovation and entrepreneurship. His inspirational story has been featured in a number of publications, including Entrepreneur magazine. His journey has brought him much financial success, but more importantly, it has afforded him the time and personal freedom to do what he believes is most important—enjoying life and his close-knit family.

RK Kliebenstein is a self-storage industry pioneer. He is an internationally renowned author and speaker with extensive experience in numerous aspects of financing, develop-ing, acquiring, and managing self-storage properties. He is an innovator whose many years of dedication and hard work have helped self-storage achieve its modern status as one of today's best investment opportunities. During his career, RK has been responsible for underwriting over $1 billion in self-storage transactions, running more than 1,000 acquisi-tion and development projects, and personally conducting due diligence on over 100 mil-lion square feet of self-storage space.

RK began his career in self-storage converting incubator space to self-storage use. He worked for both National Self Storage and Self Storage Mortgage Corp. Subsequently, RK joined the Amsdell Companies (NYSE: YSI) where he was responsible for the acquisition and integration of more than $125 million in self-storage properties. He also served on the founding executive management team of Extra Space Storage (NYSE: EXR).

Currently, RK serves as President of Coast-to-Coast Storage, one of the premier self-storage consulting firms in the world. The company provides solutions in all areas of self-storage including high level strategic consulting and business planning, feasibility studies, site selection, comprehensive development and acquisition services, property management, and financing.

Coast-To-Coast Storage is developing self-storage and RV and Boat Storage facilities throughout the United States. In addition to domestic activity, the company is currently working on projects in the U.K., France, Canada and Mexico.

SECTION ONE
UNDERSTANDING THE SELF-STORAGE BUSINESS

CHAPTER ONE

INDUSTRY OVERVIEW

THE HISTORY OF SELF-STORAGE

The roots of self-storage may be traced back to Western Europe in the late 17th century. Back then, sailors embarking in search of new lands needed a place to keep their things. In London, Parliament authorized the construction of warehouses to store these goods.

The modern era of self-storage began in Texas during the 1960s. This time the sailors were itinerant workers setting sail for offshore oil rigs along Texas's Gulf Coast. These "mini-warehouses" as self-storage facilities were originally called, soon proved their worth and by the 1970s they had begun to spread across America.

Back then, most owners considered their self-storage investments as good land banking opportunities. The term "land banking" refers to the practice of acquiring land and holding it for future use. The idea is to buy land before expanding urbanization increases its value.

Those owners planned to operate their self-storage businesses only until the underlying land could be put to better use. Over time, most have found that self-storage *is* the best use of the land.

SIZE AND NATURE OF THE MARKET

Today, self-storage is a thriving business. According to Michael T. Scanlon, Jr., President and CEO of the Self Storage Association (SSA), there are over 44,000 self-storage facilities in the United States in 2005.

Most experts agree that these facilities generated nearly $15 billion in 2004. Approximately 95 percent of these revenues came from rents. The remaining five percent resulted from the sale of miscellaneous products and services.

Despite its success, the industry remains relatively unsophisticated and highly fragmented. Today, roughly 75 percent of self-storage facilities are owned by small independent "mom and pop" operators.

In most industries of this size, bigger companies tend to consolidate, squeezing smaller players out of the market.

Consolidation is occurring in the self-storage industry. The problem for would-be consolidators has been the following: most owners find that self-storage is such a great, high cash-flow business, that they don't want to sell. As a result, the largest owner operator, Public Storage, controls only 6.0 percent of the market when determined by rentable square footage. Together, the top 50 companies control approximately 23.8 percent. (See Appendix A for a list of the top self-storage operators.)

FROM BLACK SHEEP TO BEST OF THE BUNCH

Until recently, self-storage was viewed as the black sheep of investment products. Wall Street stayed away for many reasons, including:

- The lack of a well-organized trade association

- A scarcity of detailed information about the industry

- An unglamorous image

- Negative myths regarding storage

Real estate investors followed Wall Street's lead. They preferred beautiful new trophy buildings in the center of town to old storage facilities on the outskirts or buried behind industrial parks.

So, what happened? How did self-storage investments go from being considered the black sheep to best of the bunch?

ENTER BLUE CHIP COMPANIES AND HIGHLY SOPHISTICATED OPERATORS

The turning point came in the 1990s for several reasons:

- The first meaningful data on the business began to emerge.

- The first self-storage Real Estate Investment Trusts (REITs) were formed.

- The first securitized debt was offered to self-storage investors.

- The Wall Street Journal began to identify self-storage as a lucrative business.

- Self-storage facilities were upgraded with better designs and more amenities such as heavy-duty security and climate control.

- Self-storage facilities moved to better locations, closer to town centers.

- For many self-storage facilities, continued rent increases became the norm.

- Lowest default rate of all property types.

- Industry leader, Public Storage, institutionally recognized as one of the most respected of all property REITs.

Now that the business was in vogue, investment money poured into self-storage. Development activity accelerated sharply. In less than 10 years, the number of self-storage facilities in the United States doubled. Then in May 2002, General Electric (GE) became one of the country's largest self-storage providers when it acquired over 500 Storage USA facilities, putting the first blue chip stamp of approval on the booming self-storage business.

CARVING OUT YOUR PIECE OF THE PIE

The good news is that there is still plenty of room for entrepreneurs and investors in this booming industry. This book will help you steer clear of mistakes and take the first steps towards profiting from this still fast-growing business.

CHAPTER TWO

THE INVESTMENT OPPORTUNITY

WHERE SHOULD I INVEST MONEY TODAY?

You probably hear it at every event or backyard BBQ you attend. It's the "Big Question." Where should I invest money today? Those who pose this question are really asking, "Where can I find stable and predictable returns with the least amount of risk?"

Despite the wide variety of investment options available, most prudent investors still prefer to invest in real estate and/or the stock market.

Both of these investment types have experienced periods of boom and bust. For that reason, people are often advised to diversify their investment portfolio. This involves investing in a wide range of assets such as stocks and bonds in ratios designed to spread out the various risks and produce a balanced portfolio.

Despite such strategies, it's important to remember that there's no magic bullet. Markets rise and fall, only to rise again. The cycle repeats itself. Many of those who have ridden the recent real estate wave in home prices over the past few years may have fooled themselves into thinking that meteoric rises in value will last forever. These investors are in need of a reality check and the dot-com investors of the late 1990s will be happy to provide them with one.

Our goal goes beyond traditional concepts such as diversification. It focuses on America's most popular and well-tested route to financial independence. Building wealth by investing in property is still the most successful investment for Americans. We strongly suggest that you follow the path thousands of millionaires have beaten to sizeable profits and the "The Good Life."

So, if you're looking for the most stable and predictable investments over the long term with the least amount of risk, join us as we cast an unapologetic vote for good, old-fashioned real estate.

WHY INVEST IN REAL ESTATE?

The advantages of investing in real estate include:

- Leverage

Most real estate is purchased using borrowed money. You are betting that you can earn more from the borrowed money than you spend on repaying the loan. Leverage refers to this process of creating positive cash flow using borrowed money. In real estate, leverage allows you to control (and profit from) an expensive property by making relatively small payments on a mortgage or other loan.

- Tax Advantages

Real estate investing gives you tax deductions for property taxes and interest paid on a mortgage.

- Passive Income

Are you working for your money, or is your money working for you? Real estate investments often create a steady stream of passive income that increases over time.

- Control Over Your Investments

Unlike many investments, real estate puts you in the driver's seat, firmly in control of your property.

- Appreciation

Real estate investment has consistently appreciated in value over the past 25 years.

Why Invest in Self-Storage?

As an investment, self-storage offers several advantages beyond real estate by combining the many benefits of real estate investing with those of a low-overhead, high-margin business.

The good news is that the gap between self-storage and other real estate types appears set to increase in the future as the market for storage continues to expand. Self-storage is already a large and emerging market. Despite the over 44,000 facilities in the United States, relatively few Americans have ever used self-storage. Industry sources calculate that only six percent of the U.S. population is using self-storage at any given time. Despite these low usage rates, occupancy levels typically average 85 percent to 90 percent nationwide. In some high-growth areas, occupancy rates are even higher.

In the future, the self-storage industry will continue to grow as it draws strength from several major societal, demographic and business trends. We'll begin with societal trends.

- There is a generally increasing demand for storage space.

- There is increased mobility. We tend to move around a lot and we like to take our stuff with us.

- We tend to accumulate possessions in ever-increasing numbers. Many of us find it difficult to let go of our stuff. This is especially true when items hold a nostalgic value, such as a deceased loved one's favorite chair.

- We're active and we enjoy our jet skis, boats, RVs, etc. These toys are typically large and getting larger. Many new communities do not allow these toys to be stored on the street or in front of a home.

All this stuff requires an increasing amount of storage space. Little of this demand has been met by the recent proliferation of new homes, condominiums and apartments. The majority of this new construction fails to meet the storage needs of today's families.

Then there are demographic trends:

- Many retirees downsize their primary homes only to discover that they no longer have enough storage space for their possessions.

- More and more Americans are buying second homes, increasing the demand for storage space.

- As baby boomers' kids move on to college, their parents often downsize into a smaller home. Now they need to find storage for their "stuff" as well as all the possessions left behind by college-bound kids.

- Students in college accumulate new belongings (such as computers, entertainment centers, clothes, etc.) further increasing the overall demand for storage space.

Many business trends are also contributing to the growing need for storage, including:

- The Changing Workplace

Offices are getting smaller, the workforce is becoming mobile, more and more of us are working as independent contractors.

- Small Businesses

To help reduce costs, many small businesses are moving out of large offices, opting to rent storage space and operate out of a smaller office.

- eBay® and Other Auction Businesses

These businesses are growing at a tremendous rate, increasing the demand for places to house all the "stuff" that's being bought and sold.

- Working From Home

Although more and more of us are working from home, few homes provide enough storage space to meet the needs of home offices.

SELF-STORAGE VS. THE STOCK MARKET

Stock market investors are investing in companies operated by other people who run the companies on your behalf. Self-storage investing puts you in control of how your money is spent in the pursuit of profits. Some investment advisors will claim that this loss of control is countered by the stock market's diversification. The right mix of stocks allows you to build a widely diversified portfolio of domestic and foreign companies. This diversification reduces your vulnerability to changes on Wall Street.

These experts criticize self-storage investing as putting all your eggs into one basket. However, another way to view this is to describe stock market investing as investing in a volatile market in which diversification is essential to avoid losing money when the market changes. Compared to stocks, real estate investing provides relative stability for your investment dollar.

In addition to stability, real estate offers other advantages over investing in stocks:

- Higher Returns

Self-storage tends to outperform the stock market. From 1982 to 2002, for example, the compound annual growth rate of the S&P 500 fell 1.94 percent as money invested in self-storage continued to grow.

- High Leverage

Unlike stock market investments, self-storage allows you to leverage your money. For example, if you have $1,000 to invest in the stock market you can buy only $1,000 worth of stock (unless you buy on margin). If however, you invest in self-storage you will typically take out a loan for 75 percent of the purchase price. Your $1,000 investment gives you control over $4,000 of real property.

- Other People's Money

There are many ways to raise cash for your self-storage investment. One of the best is by using other people's money or OPM for short.

When you take out a loan, you are using other people's money to help you buy or build a property. This is true whether you get a loan from your bank or raise money from a group of investors who believe in your plans and are counting on you to provide a return on their investment. Such investors are often attracted by self-storage's tendency to outperform the stock market and other real estate investments.

SELF-STORAGE VS. OTHER REAL ESTATE INVESTMENTS

While all property types offer the advantages of real estate investments, only self-storage provides the following benefits:

- Lower Development Costs

Those who choose to build self-storage facilities find that development costs for their buildings are often 30 to 50 percent less than office, retail, and apartment buildings. Modern state-of-the art properties, for example, can be built for between $40 to $60 per square foot (excluding land costs). However, rental incomes for these facilities are typically comparable to "B" grade apartments with construction costs well over $100 per square foot.

- Lower Operating Costs

Operating costs for self-storage facilities are typically less than office, retail, and apartment buildings.

- Lower Break-Even Occupancy

Lower development and operating costs make break-even occupancy ranges lower than other forms of real estate.

- Excellent Cash Flow/Liquidity

Rental rates for self-storage facilities are at or on par with other real estate investments; however, lower development and operating costs create higher profits and a greater return for investors.

- Increasing Product Demand

Occupancy levels and rental rates for stabilized self-storage facilities are near all-time highs, however, population trends, better education of mainstream consumers, the emergence of major consumer brands, and the addition of a variety of customized products and services all point to an explosion in the use of self-storage.

- Enhanced Rent Elasticity

Self-storage's month-to-month contracts mean that rental rates can be adjusted very easily. Just as with any other commodity, rents are based on supply and demand. When no further space is available, the price typically increases. A successful operator will have an occupancy level of 85 to 90 percent. When occupancy exceeds these levels, a savvy operator will increase prices. This may force some tenants to move out, but the new replacement tenants will all come in at the higher rental rates. Today's progressive self-storage operators are likely to use revenue management tools similar to those in the airline, hotel, and car rental industries to help maximize their income.

- A Recession-Resistant Business

Demand for self-storage is relatively immune to economic cycles, particularly with respect to commercial users.

- High Rate of Customer Loyalty

Self-storage tends to generate long-term, repeat customers.

- Low Frequency of Customer Visits

According to the Self Storage Association, once they've moved their possessions in, 95 percent of self-storage customers do not return to their unit until the day they move out of the facility. Compare this low "pester factor" with the number of tenant "interactions" required to operate a comparable apartment building.

- No "Single Large Customer" Problem

Unlike commercial real estate, with self-storage there's no "single large customer" problem. Self-storage space is rented on a month-to-month basis to hundreds of different customers. Most of these clients will be individuals and small business tenants. In contrast, many office and retail sites are crucially dependent on one large "flagship" client. If this client moves out, the owner is left with a large space to fill. With self-storage, no single move-out is going to cause a major problem.

- Lower Failure Rate

Self-storage has the ability to absorb economic fluctuations better than other real estate investments. As a result, self-storage has the lowest failure rate of any real estate product type.

- Excellent Liquidity

Once they reach stabilized occupancy, self-storage businesses are highly liquid assets. This means that they can be turned over quickly. In fact, well-located, properly managed facilities usually sell before they ever hit the market. A successful facility can be sold to one of the top operators or a new investor entering the industry. The challenge is finding good facilities for sale because owners are hard pressed to find a better place to invest their money. For this reason, those who invest in self-storage tend to reinvest in the business because of good returns.

- Strong Interest From Blue Chip Companies

After years of sitting on the sidelines, blue chip companies are now entering the self-storage market in search of increased cash flow. One of the first to enter the market was General Electric (GE). As more blue chip companies and other sophisticated operators buy into the industry or expand their market share, midsize operators and well-located independent facilities have become increasingly attractive acquisition targets.

To summarize, when compared with traditional investments including other real estate property types, self-storage offers many advantages to the prudent investor. A well-located and well-managed self-storage facility can be a stable and predictable investment providing high cash flow with relatively few maintenance demands.

As you'll learn in the upcoming chapters, self-storage can also be a largely "hands-off" investment. Firms are now available to provide turn-key solutions for investors in such areas as market analysis, site selection, development, acquisition, and property management. These companies can help you get into the business and/or manage your self-storage facility, freeing you up to enjoy high investment returns with a minimum of day-to-day involvement.

CHAPTER THREE
SEPARATING FACT FROM FICTION

Before we discuss getting started in self-storage, let's double-check to make sure that this business is right for you. We've already mentioned that self-storage has been a thriving industry for the past several years. We also noted that, until recently, self-storage has flown under the radar of most investors.

But that's not the case today—the "secret is out" on self-storage. Various capital sources and fierce competition have changed the business significantly. As a result, many of the things you have heard in the past about self-storage may no longer hold true.

In this chapter, we'll take a look at some of those common myths and help you to separate fact from fiction.

COMMON MYTHS ABOUT SELF-STORAGE
The following is a list of common myths that you may have heard about self-storage along with our responses to each one.

1. "If You Build It, They Will Come."

For years this saying was true in many places because there were very few self-storage facilities. Today however, self-storage has been "discovered." For the first time we are seeing competition in virtually every market. What's more, this competition is coming from very sophisticated operators. In addition to the general increase in competition, we've also begun to see overbuilding in many areas.

With this in mind, we suggest replacing the old saying, "If you build it, they will come," with a new saying: "If you build it in the right location, provide the right mix of products and services for your market, and your customers need it, maybe they will come."

2. "Self-Storage Is A Really Simple Business."

Again, while this may have seemed true in the past, because of the increased competition today, self-storage is no longer a simple business. It is in fact a very challenging and increasingly sophisticated business.

To succeed, owners need to work smarter every step of the way. Developers need to be more precise when considering where to build new facilities. Buyers of existing product need to conduct thorough due diligence to make sure they are buying a facility that can compete over the long term in their markets, and that the local markets are not overbuilt.

Managers need to do everything possible to supply the right products and services, and run their facilities well if they are to maximize profits and beat out their competition for new customers.

3. "I've Been Successful With Other Property Types So This Should Be Easy."

We hear this one all the time. Those who have enjoyed success owning rental, retail, or industrial properties often think of self-storage as a relatively easy business. As we noted above, nothing could be further from the truth. Self-storage is truly a different animal. It's just as much a business enterprise as it is a real estate investment. Most commercial and industrial brokers don't specialize in the industry and truly understand this unique property type.

Many of these people develop or acquire a facility without taking the time to learn how to manage their new business. As a result, they lose money and are often forced to sell their properties at a loss.

4. "Everyone's Making Money In Self-Storage."

This is perhaps the biggest myth. There may have been a time when it was true but that has changed. Every week, we see people who are having problems with their businesses. Most of these problems can be traced to a failure to do proper planning and homework up-front.

Those who get into a project before conducting careful feasibility studies or appropriate due diligence are setting themselves up for a host of problems. These include building or buying in the wrong location, investing in a market that is overbuilt, and not managing the property correctly.

5. "This Is A Cheap Business To Get Into."

One common mistake involves failing to prepare accurate budgets for self-storage projects. This is due to the old myth that getting into the storage business is relatively cheap.

Like many other industries, self-storage is a highly capital-intensive business. The process of planning, building, leasing-up, and properly managing a self-storage facility can be lengthy and very expensive, and lease-up of new facilities are taking longer.

Years ago, the cost of land and materials for many self-storage investors was relatively low. This was due to the fact that storage was most commonly found on cheap land at the outskirts of town or in the back of an industrial park. Today, storage has moved closer to , increasing land costs. The costs of building materials have also increased.

New demand by emerging nations has helped push up the prices of most building materials including concrete, steel, and lumber.

In addition to higher land and building costs, storage operators are also being forced to offer a variety of products and services. These additional amenities and offerings cost money to build or stock. For example, adding climate control and enhancing security systems increases costs.

Finally, the lease-up time for new projects has increased significantly. Five years ago a project would commonly be fully leased within 18 to 24 months. Today, in many areas, developers face a 36 to 48 month lease-up period due to increased competition and the amount of available product. This means that they need to carry the financial load of a project for a longer period.

6. "I Already Own the Land, So I Can't Lose."

Many people assume that the plot of land they already own will work for self-storage. We see this mistake frequently. All too often, these owners rush to build self-storage on their land without doing their homework. These facilities either sit empty, or fail to generate enough revenue to pay the loan on the building improvements. As a result, these individuals end up losing their land and their businesses.

THE RIGHT REASONS TO GET INTO THE BUSINESS

When we studied the most successful people in the industry, we found they shared a few common characteristics and approached the business in very similar ways:

- They were well capitalized.

- They had built great teams of experienced self-storage professionals to help them every step of the way.

- They were tenacious, thorough, and insistent on doing their homework in a timely fashion.

- They never went into a deal without having an extensive understanding of the market, including a very good grasp of supply and demand in the local area.

- They were very well prepared. They believed they needed to be prepared in order to overcome everyone else's lack of knowledge regarding the industry. As a result, they were able to overcome objections from private investors, lending institutions, municipalities, and the like. They made sure that they were better educated than these groups in all aspects.

- Many came to the self-storage business with successful records as real estate developers or investors.

- Many had experience managing rental property.

- Several had successful track records as entrepreneurs.

I'm Sold! How Do I Get Started?

If after careful consideration you still believe this industry is right for you, the next question is, "How do I get started?" There are several resources that can help you, including:

- Self Storage Association

This industry organization provides resources and can connect you with the right professionals.

- Industry Trade Magazines

Publications such as *Mini-Storage Messenger* and *Inside Self Storage* also provide educational products and services related to the self-storage industry.

It's also important to begin building a strong team. The right team usually includes the following professionals:

- An attorney

- An accountant

- Real estate agents to identify suitable land that is for sale

- Self-storage brokers to find existing properties for sale

- Feasibility and due diligence experts to advise on opportunities and deals

- Architects and developers who specialize in self-storage

- Construction experts and building material suppliers

- Financing experts to help with loans and equity

- Insurance professionals to protect your investment

OVERCOMING BARRIERS TO ENTRY

Getting started in self-storage is not as easy as it was in the industry's early days. Back then, would-be owners had only to compile a list of target properties and then choose the one they liked the best (See Appendix B for a Sample Target Property List).

Today self-storage is recognized as a great business opportunity by institutions and sophisticated investors. This has led to significant competition for the relatively small number of stores that hit the market. As a result, the past few years have seen the emergence of a classic seller's market.

When good buys are scarce, patience is king. People who are just getting started in the business must avoid getting caught up in the frenzy. It's far better to keep looking for the right property than to rush into a dubious deal. Remember the old adage, "In real estate you make your money on the buy."

It's not just more difficult to buy in today's market. It's also more difficult to build. There's strong competition for the dwindling number of really good affordable locations. Moreover, for the first time, the industry is not just competing for space on the outskirts of town; it's now competing for sites in the heart of the city. This means that self-storage developers are going head-to-head with office, retail, multifamily, and mixed-use developers. Because self-storage doesn't typically generate significant sales tax revenue for the city, most cities favor these competing businesses, tilting the playing field in favor of office, retail and other developments.

NEXT STEPS

Overcoming these and other challenging barriers to entry usually means assembling the right team of self-storage professionals, and creating and executing a well thought-out plan. In the next section we will provide you with several specific steps for overcoming these barriers to entry and launching a successful self-storage venture.

SECTION TWO
HOW TO INVEST IN SELF-STORAGE

CHAPTER FOUR

MARKET ANALYSIS

Market analysis forms the bedrock of your single most important decision: determining where to buy or locate your facility. No other decision will have as great an impact on your future success or failure.

In this chapter we'll discuss how to conduct a thorough market analysis. Specifically, we'll show you how to identify potential self-storage customers and the reasons behind their purchase decisions. We'll also help you define your target markets, analyze households and migration patterns, understand self-storage supply and demand, and select your best site.

We'll begin with ways of defining the available market for self-storage.

WHO USES SELF-STORAGE?

Self-storage is a demand-driven, activity-driven business, which thrives on today's increasingly mobile population.

The industry breaks today's self-storage customers into four main groups
1) Residential, 2) Business, 3) Students, and 4) Military.

The following is a breakdown of these customer groups:

- Residential Customers

Residential customers make up approximately 75 percent of the self-storage customer mix. On average, residential clients will rent storage for a one-year period.

Residential customers usually rent storage because of a lifestyle change triggered by a major event such as:

- ~ Marriage/Divorce
- ~ Birth/Death
- ~ Purchase/Sale of a home
- ~ New job/Laid off
- ~ Relocation
- ~ Children leaving home
- ~ Retirement

~ Bankruptcy
~ Natural disasters

It is interesting to note that 70 percent of the time, women make the final decision to rent storage. Women are also more likely to spend time shopping around for the best storage deals.

• Business Customers

Business customers comprise approximately 20 percent of the customer mix. Costs for business and commercial space are escalating. As a result, many small businesses would rather put extra furniture or boxes in storage and avoid paying to rent expensive office space.

In addition to soaring costs, business and commercial customers often rent storage to deal with a variety of events, including:

~ Business expansion due to economic upswings
~ Business contraction caused by economic downturns
~ Fluctuating inventory levels
~ Increases in the number of documents and records the IRS requires businesses to preserve
~ Bankruptcy
~ Natural disasters

Business customers are preferred tenants because they tend to:

~ Pay more
~ Stay longer (two years on average)
~ Stay put despite rent increases

• Students

Students make up approximately three percent of the average customer mix. Students tend to stay for the shortest period of time (approximately four months).

This is a seasonal business with students renting mostly in the summer months. Whenever possible, plan to reduce these cyclical income fluctuations by balancing student rentals with residential and business clients.

• Military

On average, members of the armed services comprise about two percent of self-storage customers. Like residential customers, they tend to leave their furniture and other belongings in storage for some 12 months at a time.

In the military, a promotion often means relocating to a new base. This can create a short-term need for self-storage until belongings can be moved to the new posting. Soldiers heading overseas on active duty need long-term storage for the duration of their tour of duty. Oftentimes, this includes storage for vehicles.

Be sure to clearly identify any tenant who is in the military. The best way to do this is at the time an application form is accepted. Military personnel can be shipped out to destinations anywhere in the world on very short notice, and they aren't always given sufficient time to set all their business affairs in order. With this in mind, you might want to consider extending extra courtesies, such as an extended late payment notification procedure to our men and women in uniform.

DEFINING YOUR TARGET MARKET

Self-storage is a local business. The average facility typically defines its market as the three- to five-mile mile radius (or 10-minute driving range) surrounding that facility. According to the Self Storage Association, 95 percent of the average facility's tenants either live or work within that 3-5 mile radius. As the number of facilities increases in a market, the competitive radius tends to decrease.

This relatively small size of the target market often surprises people. Many insist that their potential market is bigger, but they are usually wrong. If they act on these mistaken beliefs, they will build or buy in the wrong location. It's important to remember that what works in one storage market won't necessarily work a few minutes down the road.

Because target markets are so small, begin your search for the right site by defining a small, finite area. Searching in California, for example, is too vague, as is Los Angeles. Carving out a specific area of a suburb in Los Angeles is much more practical.

In doing your research, it may be helpful to consider how large institutions select a market or specific location. (See Appendix C for a listing of Institutional Grade Criteria.)

ANALYZING HOUSEHOLDS AND MIGRATION PATTERNS

When studying a market you should get to know its population trends, demographics, household composition, and migration patterns.

Self-storage thrives on mobility. As a result, an area with many renters is often preferable to one full of homeowners because renters tend to move more frequently. You should also look for areas with many businesses.

It always helps when potential customers can afford to pay for renting self-storage. Determine your potential customers' financial standing by analyzing a variety of demographic characteristics including age, gender, and household income. A few of the demographic markers you should evaluate in your target market include:

- The Mix of Renters vs. Homeowners

Seek out markets with a high percentage of renters vs. homeowners.

- Unmarried vs. Married

Most storage operators prefer areas with a higher proportion of unmarried people. Single tenants tend to move more than married folks, thus triggering a higher demand for storage.

- Age

It used to be that young adults in their twenties and thirties moved much more than older Americans. But today, everyone is moving. The trend towards older Americans becoming more mobile has been buoyed by an increase in baby boomers buying second homes. As a general rule of thumb, look for areas where the average resident is more than 30 years of age.

- Income

The minimum median income of your target market should range from $45,000 to $50,000 per year. (Median income is the middle income in the entire range of incomes. For example, if there were 100 salaries, the median salary would be the wage paid to the person ranked 50th).

It's also important to study migration patterns in the area. Are people moving in or moving out? Choose those areas where population is steady or increasing. Ideally we want to be in places that are enjoying population growth rates of at least three to five percent per year.

That being said, there are some locations that work very well for storage even though they're not seeing significant growth in population. These areas include urban locations that have been completely built out, so there is no room for growth. In this type of area, the most important thing to consider is whether the population is stable or decreasing for some reason.

UNDERSTANDING SELF-STORAGE SUPPLY AND DEMAND
One of the self-storage industry's ongoing debates focuses on over-building or market saturation, as it is known in financial circles. This debate is ongoing because we have

few yardsticks for determining when a particular market has reached equilibrium in terms of supply and demand.

As competition in our industry increases, understanding supply and demand becomes more and more important. In the future, we'll see self-storage facilities running into trouble because they're situated in overbuilt markets. You can minimize this risk by understanding self-storage supply and demand. One simple piece of advice would be to avoid buying or developing in suburban areas where there are few barriers to entry because others can build in your market area with relative ease. This is one instance where high barriers to entry can work in your favor by protecting you from excessive supply in your marketplace.

Analyzing supply and demand is not yet an exact science. Even experts disagree about the best way to measure supply and demand. Let's look at two popular approaches.

• Square Foot Per Capita

At first glance, determining market saturation by measuring square feet per capita seems very logical. The reality is that this approach may be very dangerous.

The method of square foot per capita measures the number of available square feet per person in a defined area. In late 2004 for example, according to the *2005 Self-Storage Almanac*, the U.S. national average of available self-storage space was 4.94 square feet per individual. Many industry observers urge caution when applying this square foot per capita metric to decide for example, where to locate a new facility. They argue that it oversimplifies. Las Vegas for instance, has the highest level of available storage (8.5 square feet per capita). New York has the lowest (0.73). Yet both markets report occupancies at the 88-percent level.

Given these figures, which city would you prefer to compete in? It's hard to say. A better yardstick would compare a stringent, exhaustive count of square footage with the very latest occupancy rates. There's no glut of square feet per capita until there are too many square feet, as measured by occupancy. In other words, the number of square feet per capita has to be quantified by occupancy.

Occupancy only drops in response to one of two conditions: Supply exceeds demand, or rates are not reduced enough to sustain occupancy levels when in an overbuilt market.

• Occupancy/Vacancy Patterns

This approach attempts to measure demand by concentrating on patterns of occupancy and vacancy. These patterns will indicate whether vacancies are increasing, decreasing or stable. As a general rule of thumb, enter markets when they reach 90-percent occupancy rates (assuming that no new developments or expansions are about to increase supply)

When considering this metric, it's important to distinguish between physical and economic occupancy. Physical occupancy refers to the number of units or square feet rented, without regard to rates. Economic occupancy is a more accurate metric. It measures the rents that these units are actually generating, factoring in all discounts and incentives and delinquent rents due. This is a crucial distinction, much like the difference between projected and actual budget figures or proforma versus actual numbers. Never make an offer based on physical occupancy figures. Seek out the economic occupancy data.

Many experts subscribe to this theory. They suggest that if a high level of discounting exists and rental rate growth has been stagnant, then demand may be soft. Developers should be cautious about markets where there are stores that don't enjoy high (above 90 percent) occupancy levels.

Since measuring supply and demand is not yet an exact science, we prefer to look at a combination of both methods. Obviously occupancy rates are the most important consideration. Before we enter a market, we need to see occupancy in all that market's facilities running at 88 percent and above, an absence of new construction, no new expansion planned, and annual population increases of three percent or more. As mentioned earlier, we may consider certain locations that aren't experiencing significant population growth if they're stable urban locations.

SELECTING THE BEST SITE

Congratulations! You've identified a market that has a combination of the right demographic mix, healthy population growth patterns, and a strong demand for storage. Now it's time to focus on selecting the ideal site for your self-storage facility.

What makes a really good site? In urban markets look for locations with:

- Acceptable zoning

- Appropriate pricing

- Very high traffic counts

- Dense neighborhoods

- High median household income levels

- High visibility

- Proximity to major thoroughfares

- A location between residential and business areas, close to Main Street

- A low number of turns (to drive onto the property)

- Barriers to entry for competitors

It's also very important in today's competitive environment to look for sites that have substantial barriers to entry. Some of the biggest mistakes we see today are experienced by owners who develop or acquire a self-storage facility in an area where it is easy for competition to saturate the market, which usually leads to higher vacancy and lower rental rates.

You will typically be looking for approximately two to three acres of land. As land costs have risen, these plots have become harder to find. This land shortage has forced people to build multistory self-storage facilities. Building smaller facilities may still pencil out profitability on higher priced land assuming that you're able to charge higher rents.

One hot trend in urban markets is converting an existing space to self-storage use. Such conversions often offer the following advantages:

- A superior location

- Faster speed to market because no time is spent on building a facility from the ground up

It's important, however, to exercise caution. Conversion projects (which can seem very straightforward at the initial planning stage) often run into crippling cost overruns that can turn them upside down.

Popular self-storage conversion targets include:

- Conversion of obsolete warehouses

- Car dealerships

- "Dark" big boxes (such as Wal-Mart® or K-Mart® stores)

- Strip centers

- Grocery stores

- Drive-in theaters

- Bowling alleys

- Skating rinks

- Home improvement centers

- Schools

- Theaters

- Airports

- Government buildings

Suburban markets can be more tricky and risky than urban settings. The main challenge is that suburban markets don't have as many people, so there is less demand for storage.

A related challenge in suburban markets involves zoning. In some cases, zoning restrictions are less stringent. So, if one facility is performing well, it's relatively easy for a competitor to build right next door or across the street. As a result, suburban markets have a tendency to quickly become overbuilt. This, of course, undermines the original developer's investment and hard work.

On the other hand, we have seen some suburban markets that are totally opposed to self-storage. Their attitude is that they don't want self-storage businesses in their own back yards. The key thing is to do your homework and find out exactly how the local planning commission feels about self-storage in your area.

Proximity to colleges can be good, but student business is cyclical. Students tend to store their things in the summer and move out when classes start back up in the fall Make sure that there's a strong base of alternative tenants to rent to after the students return to school.

Locations close to military bases can make good sites. While military personnel tend to make excellent tenants, watch out for base closures if they become the largest portion of your customer base. In general, military personnel make great long-term tenants. It should be noted that in the past, the military has discussed building self-storage for its personnel on base. Fortunately, the Self Storage Association was able to confer with the military. The organization succeeded in convincing the military that it was in everyone's best interests to keep self-storage privatized. However, some branches of the military may reconsider building their own storage facilities on bases.

One last point when it comes to military customers is that you must be aware of their active duty status as the Servicemembers Civil Relief Act prohibits their goods from being sold at a lien sale should they be shipped overseas.

In summary, self-storage will work in a wide variety of locations—both destination sites and local neighborhoods. In fact, a location's proximity to colleges and universities, multi-family communities, shopping centers, and large employers can help signal good candidates for self-storage locations.

In this chapter we've shown you what to look for in a good self-storage market. We've emphasized finding the right site in terms of demographic mix, healthy population growth patterns, and a strong, growing demand for self-storage. Now, it's time to focus on ways of making money from your facility.

CHAPTER FIVE

PRODUCT ANALYSIS

Self-storage facilities generate income from two main sources. The largest is of course, rental income representing approximately 95 percent of revenues. The other five percent of income flows from administrative fees, late charges and the sale of miscellaneous products and services. This chapter explores these revenue sources in detail.

HOW DO SELF-STORAGE BUSINESSES GENERATE REVENUE?

Self-storage businesses have drastically changed over the years. So have their locations. As the stores moved closer to Main Street, the towns and cities have demanded more in terms of "look and feel" to ensure that they blend into the community. The stores themselves have boosted revenues by offering more and more products and services.

When reviewing its own growth, the industry identifies three major generations of development. Each differs in terms of the types of buildings, products and services offered. We'll briefly discuss each generation in turn so you can understand how your facility stacks up, and what you may need to add to it in order to provide the best products and get the highest possible rents from your customers.

First Generation (1965 to 1988) - In the early days of self-storage, metal buildings with garage doors were built in industrial parks, or on land that would otherwise be unused. In urban settings, old warehouses or manufacturing plants were converted for self-storage use by putting up dividing walls, and creating a small office. A number of suburban and rural facilities operated without on-site employees. Prospective tenants simply called a posted phone number to rent a room or shed in what was often termed a mini-warehouse.

This lead to what became known as "first generation" mini-storage facilities characterized by:

- Chain-link fencing

- Unpaved driveways

- Manual gates

- Orange doors

- Metal buildings, stick frame

- Typically owned by independent owner-operators, referred to as the "Mom and Pops" of the industry

- Small 10-by-10 offices commonly connected to (or inside) a small apartment where the manager lived

Second generation (1989 to 1993) - The second generation of self-storage was characterized by many improvements, including:

- Sites gained more prominent locations closer to customers.

- Metal framing with block structures was used.

- Driveways were almost always paved.

- Buildings were often situated along the self-storage facility's perimeter in the so-called "fortress style."

- Offices added retail areas selling , tapes, boxes and moving supplies on well-lit, highly visible racks.

- Owners reacted to increases in land costs by building up, creating multistory sites rather than building out across the land.

- Technology began to play its part with the introduction of personal computers, security systems with CCTV (Closed Circuit Television) cameras, site-management software, etc.

- Customers gained entry through electronically controlled gates.

- On-site managers became more professional as larger companies developed multi-store operations.

- Real Estate Investment Trusts (REITs) were formed.

- Several large suppliers began to emerge as industry leaders grew beyond the 100-store mark.

- The industry developed its own trade organization, the Self Storage Association.

In the middle part of this era, many enterprising owners found a way to benefit from the sheer newness of this property type. They applied for planning permission to build in prominent locations. These owners were often given permission to build in these great locations by zoning officials who lacked experience with self-storage facilities.

In the later days of the second generation, between 1990 and 1993 access to capital was limited, but Wall Street was about to discover this lucrative industry. By 1995, capital was readily available and storage was moving toward state-of-the art construction, technology, and management, which led to the current generation of facilities.

Today's state-of-the-art self-storage facilities are very different from their predecessors. Many of these stores, for example, have responded to zoning regulations by adopting disguises. They don't even look like self-storage facilities. Other features include:

- High-traffic and high-visibility locations

- Great signage

- Upscale locations in retail centers or close to destination locations such as a Wal-Mart or Home Depot

- Co-located with car washes, strip centers, and low-level retail stores

- Sizes ranging from 60,000 to 85,000 square feet

- Video surveillance with tape/hard-drive backups, fully-computerized offices, and at least two computers on site

- Motion-detector lighting in the hallways

- Zoned temperature and humidity control

- Automatic sliding doors at loading gates

- Offices comparable to an upscale retail store

- Brightly-lit, business-oriented customer areas

- A dress code with employees in uniforms or company shirts

- Relatively easy to finance and sell

RENTAL INCOME AND LEASE STRUCTURE

As previously mentioned, most self-storage income is generated by renting storage units. This source accounts for some 95 percent of revenues.

One important way to maximize your rental income is by developing the right mix of unit sizes, or, as industry professionals call it, the right unit mix. Unit mix refers to the variety of different unit sizes offered. The correct unit mix, which should always be based on a thorough understanding of your customers' needs, is unique for each facility.

One way to get the unit mix right is by hiring an experienced property management company to conduct a thorough analysis. This company will survey the local competition's rental rates, occupancy levels, and the like, and will then advise you on the right unit mix. Taking local market conditions into account, the company might, for example, recommend the following sample unit mix:

SAMPLE UNIT MIX

UNIT SIZE	PERCENT DISTRIBUTION
5X10	20%
10X10	25%
10X15	20%
10X20	25%
10X25	10%

If you move ahead on the basis of this consultant's recommendation, monitor your rental phase closely for examples of oversupply or shortages. Use this information to adjust the average unit size as needed to meet demand. If for example, your 10-by-15s are empty while renters are clamoring for 10-by-10s, you might be able to move partitions within units to create more 10-by-10s and fewer 10-by-15s.

If you're developing a large self-storage facility, it may be possible to build and rent out units in phases. This will allow you to adjust the unit mix in subsequent buildings.

If you provide the right products for your market, you are usually able to charge a sizable premium. Consider for example, the average difference in rents climate control makes in the following rental unit according to the *2005 Self-Storage Almanac*:

SAMPLE UNIT MIX

10X10 RENTAL UNIT	AVERAGE MONTHLY RENT
Climate Control Rental Unit	$101.22 Per Month
Non-Climate Control Unit	$ 79.87 Per Month
	21.10% Difference

In general, self-storage leases are always month-to-month leases. This works in the facility's favor as it allows the owner to change the contract and increase rents whenever needed. The downside to short-term lease contracts involves banks and lending institutions. These stalwart financial bodies prefer the "stability" of long-term contracts.

RV AND BOAT STORAGE

Providing RV and boat storage can be a cost-effective way to benefit from today's boom in boat and recreational vehicle ownership. How big is this boom? Consider that there are approximately 10 million RVs on the highway. Many of them are no doubt towing some of the 12 million boats registered in the U.S.

To date, boat and RV sales have been relatively immune to a weak economy. Thanks to their popularity amongst baby boomer families and retirees, sales are expected to continue to increase over coming years. Many RV buyers are able to enjoy a tax break by classifying their vehicle as a "second home" and living in it for a minimum of 14 days each year.

The opportunities for RV and boat storage in our industry are tremendous. Few owners use these large, expensive vehicles every day. When standing idle, such machines require serious storage. Security is crucial, as is shelter from inclement weather.

Adequate storage can be hard to find. Few modern driveways have extra space for storing RVs or large speedboats on trailers, and in many communities, street parking requires the owner to move the vehicle at least once a week. In many developments, the long-term street parking of boats and RVs is specifically banned.

Boats can be stored at marinas, but these berths are often costly and hard to find. Worst of all, from the owners' viewpoint, marina storage leaves their expensive boats exposed to the elements.

If this sounds like an opportunity, make a start by checking the local demographics. Look for a high ratio of retirees. Then check for recreational areas. Are you close to good fishing? Perhaps there are horse trails or scenic highways within an easy drive? Seeing what the competition is offering will also help to assess potential demand. Check the *Yellow Pages* for listings of RV and boat dealers.

If you decide to get into this business, the easiest way is by dedicating part of an existing facility to boat and RV storage. At the other extreme, you could build a storage property exclusively for items such as boats, RVs, box trailers, and fifth-wheel travel trailers. Whatever your choice, the good news is that compared with most real estate construction costs, building storage space for boats and vehicles is relatively inexpensive.

At the simplest entry level, you could offer a gated parking lot with gravel parking. For a step up, add concrete slabs with canopies to block the sun's damaging rays. To attract top dollar tenants, consider enclosed units with locked roll-up doors.

Increase storage flexibility by offering a mix of uncovered, semi-covered, and fully enclosed spaces.

Additional products and services would include:

- Separate entry and exit gates

- Dump stations

- Vehicle washing/repair

- Electrical outlets to keep batteries charged

- Transportation to local lakes and other popular destinations

To summarize, catering to the booming market for RV and boat self-storage can be extremely profitable. Conversion of an existing site or new construction is relatively simple and inexpensive, maintenance is minimal, and there is very little competition for this potentially lucrative market in the right areas.

Miscellaneous Products and Services

Although the individual dollar amounts may seem small, self-storage facilities make a significant proportion of their income from miscellaneous sources. These include administrative fees for services rendered to clients and late charges levied when tenants forget to pay their rents on time. As always, these charges should be tailored to your target customers.

Considering which miscellaneous products and services to offer is not a trivial task. You've got to do your homework so that you know what's important to your specific customers. It wouldn't be a good idea for example, to offer temperature- and humidity-controlled wine storage in a blue-collar neighborhood.

Remember that customers tend to patronize those self-storage facilities that best meet their needs. The right mix of products and services can increase customer retention, and may even translate into a greater tolerance for rent increases, resulting in higher rental rates.

The miscellaneous products and services with the greatest potential impact in these areas include:

- Products Such As Boxes, Packing Materials, Locks And Tapes

Many companies supply these essentials directly to the industry. They're also available as either generic or private label products.

- Moving Truck Rentals

Trucks can be provided in partnership with a moving truck vendor such as U-Haul or leased directly (leasing your own vehicle can be surprisingly cost-effective). This truck is then rented out or loaned to tenants for free. Typically the facility will employ its own driver and provide the entire service as a value-added incentive.

- Tenant Storage Insurance

Many companies specialize in providing tenant insurance directly to the industry.

- Shipping Services

Help your customers interface with the U.S. Postal Service, FedEx or UPS.

- Mailboxes

More and more self-storage facilities are considering providing mailbox services.

Customers always appreciate anything free. One winning strategy may be to offer new customers free use of a moving truck. Business customers might be favorably impressed with free use of a conference room. These are small costs that can go a long way in enhancing the way your clients feel about doing business with you.

Remember that today's customers are sophisticated. They expect a wide variety of ancillary products and services. As always, self-storage is a very local business. What works in one market may not work in another. Indeed, a successful strategy may fail in a second location just a few minutes away.

Be sure to thoroughly test-drive any goods and services before offering them to your customers. If you sell tape, for example, try using the product yourself. You'll quickly find that there are different grades of tape quality. I once purchased tape from a local self-storage store. I also ordered tape from Staples®. The self-storage tape was the worst! It gummed up the tape gun and did not adhere well. As a result, I ran short on tape, and I can assure you that I ordered replacement tape from Staples. It was more expensive, and less convenient to purchase, but the quality spoke for itself. The next time I was in the self-storage store, I asked the manager if differing qualities of tape were stocked. She told me that different grades were available, but they only carried the cheapest. Enough said?

Consider these questions when planning a miscellaneous product and services sales strategy:

- Where should I purchase the inventory?

- How do I handle defective merchandise?

- How much floor space will I need?

- How will my software treat the sales?

- Do I feature the product on my Web site?

- Do I post prices on the Web site?

- Do I include the products on my sign?

Whenever you offer goods or services for sale, remember to set up ways to track inventory and thereby your success rate. Retailers typically measured sales on a "per square foot basis" but there's no reason to stop at one metric. Also check methods such as:

- Sales per store

- Sales vs. rents

- Sales vs. total space

- Sales vs. occupied space

- Sales against total units

- Sales per staff member

- Sales per new customer (lease)

- Weekly and monthly sales growth

Most importantly, turn these figures into meaningful management data. Know which products and services are selling. Figure out what's working for you in this area at this specific time of year. Identify the best salespeople on your team. Base your decisions on facts and figures, not assumptions and guesswork.

When considering products and services, you can often gain a competitive advantage by thinking "outside the box". Never forget that your goal is to provide products and services that will work in your specific market with your target customers.

NEXT GENEREATION FACILITIES ...
NEXT GENERATION INCOME STREAMS

If present trends continue, tomorrow's self-storage facilities will almost certainly be highly sophisticated operations offering a wide range of products and services. A few examples of these products and services include:

- Offices with amenities such as rental phones and Internet connectivity

- Meeting and conference rooms

- Coffee and sandwich shops

- Mixed-use options such as on-site stores such as Starbucks, Subway®, or FedExKinko'ssm

- Pick-up and delivery boxes

- Pick-up and delivery moving services

- Record storage and management

- Locations attached to a car wash

- Document shredding

- Museum quality storage

- Fur storage

- Seasonal clothing storage (cedar-lined)

- Data storage

- Point of delivery (short-term inventory storage)

- Stores managed with technology, not people

CHAPTER SIX

OPERATING EXPENSES

In the last chapter we discussed rental income and ways of boosting that income by providing the right unit mix along with added products and services. Now we take a look at operating expenses—the costs of generating this income.

STANDARD OPERATING COSTS

Well-run self-storage facilities have lower operating costs than other types of real estate and general business investments. As a general rule of thumb, major operating expenses for a self-storage facility should run between 32 to 35 percent of gross income. This percentage will vary based on several factors, including:

- Facility Size

Larger facilities offer greater economies of scale. No matter how large or small the self-storage facility, it still requires someone "on the gate." Compared to the smaller facility, the larger facility's expenses for that employee will represent a lower percentage of gross income.

- Number Of Facilities In The Same Market Under Single Ownership

Advertising, marketing, labor, and other costs can be shared between two or more facilities.

MAJOR EXPENSES

Major expenses for a self-storage facility can typically be broken down into the following categories:

- Salaries and Related Items

- Management Fees

- Property Taxes

- Advertising and *Yellow Pages*

- Repairs and Maintenance

- Utilities

- Office Supplies, Postage, and Printing

- Professional Fees

- Insurance

- Marketing and Promotion

- Miscellaneous

HOW TO AVOID COMMON MISTAKES WHEN CREATING A BUDGET

When it comes to creating a budget, new owners frequently underestimate operating costs in such key areas as:

- Salaries

In addition to competitive salaries, provision must be made for extras such as bonuses, incentives, retirement benefits, health insurance, taxes, worker's compensation, and unemployment insurance.

- Taxes

These include property tax, along with state, local and municipal taxes.

- *Yellow Pages*

The cost of *Yellow Page* is often a surprise to first-time buyers. In addition to the size of the ad (quarter-, half-, full-page, or double-truck ads) there may also be a charge for placement. Good *Yellow Page* placement is so important to a self-storage business that some facilities have actually been bought primarily for their historical rights to premium ad placement. Note that owners of multiple sites can save money by consolidating their ad buys.

- Property Management

Property management is one of the most important expenses to build into your budget. It's essential to spend whatever it takes to ensure good property management. No other element makes such an essential contribution to success, so don't skimp. It helps if you can avoid thinking of property management expenditures as an expense item.

Instead, view them as an investment that you're putting back into your business.

An experienced third-party property management company will relieve you of all the facility's day-to-day on site responsibilities. This company will take full responsibility in such areas as personnel, , and accounting. In fact, once you've hired a good property management company you're only required to do one more thing: stay at home and collect your check.

In self-storage, property management companies typically charge a fee that is equal to between six to eight percent of your facility's gross income. This is a higher figure than normally charged for managing other property types. The higher pricing is largely a function of supply and demand. Today, while there are a growing number of expert property management companies that specialize in self-storage, these companies are pursued by a large number of owners seeking assistance. The gap between supply and demand has further lengthened in recent years as competition in the self-storage industry has intensified.

Consider hiring a property-management company if you:

- Are new to the business

- Own multiple properties

- Don't want to handle management duties yourself

Note that, if you are just getting started in the business, most banks will require third-party management as a prerequisite for financing.

SAMPLE PROFIT AND LOSS STATEMENT

Appendix D presents a Sample Profit/Loss Statement for a 50,000-square-foot self-storage facility that is renting space at $1 per square foot.

As you can see in the Sample Profit/Loss Statement, rental income represents 95 percent of gross income. Miscellaneous income including products and services like tape, boxes, packing materials, and sign up and late fees represent the remaining five percent of gross income.

A facility is considered fully rented or leased up at 85- to 90-percent occupancy. For the purposes of this example, we'll assume 90-percent occupancy.

The expenses listed for each category are based on national averages reported by self-storage operators. The actual figures are shown along with the percentage of gross income each line item represents.

Taking this facility's income and subtracting its expenses will give you the store's net operating income (NOI) before debt service. The term "debt service" refers to loan payments.

A facility's profit (or loss) can be computed by subtracting debt service obligations from (before debt service).

NEXT STEPS

Now that you have a clear understanding of how to generate revenue from a self-storage business, and the costs associated with generating that revenue, let's move on to the next step. In the next chapter we will begin to discuss how you can get into the self-storage business. Specifically, we'll try to help you answer one very important question: Should I build or should I buy?

CHAPTER SEVEN
HOW TO DEVELOP A SELF-STORAGE FACILITY

Building a facility to your own specifications is often called "development." A developer is a private investor who initiates and supervises all aspects of this process, including site selection, entitlement, planning, building, financing, management, advertising and lease up. Before describing the role of the developer in detail, we'll consider one very important question: Do you want to be a developer?

UNDERSTANDING THE RISKS VS. REWARDS

One of the biggest questions facing those seeking to invest in self-storage is always, "Should I build or should I buy?" It is impossible to answer that question without understanding the risks and rewards of these two very different strategies.

There is usually less risk in buying an existing facility than there is when setting out to build your own self-storage facility. Stores are often sold after they have reached stabilization. The buyer is paying for a store with a "proven" market and track record.

Historically speaking, self-storage physical occupancies don't significantly erode over time. What's more, as the years go by, rental rates will tend to increase, producing higher gross incomes, and ultimately increased profits and value. The only real downside to buying a store is that buyers who fail to do their homework can end up owning someone else's problems—the types of problems that are typically expensive to fix.

"Profit" is often described as the reward for taking risks. Those who decide to build their own self-storage facilities often end up with a nice profit, assuming that they avoid making any major mistakes.

As many happy owner/developers will attest, developing self-storage facilities can be an extremely profitable undertaking. Building your own store offers many advantages. Developers are free to choose a location far from competitors. The cost to buy land and develop is usually significantly lower than the price of acquiring an existing self-storage facility. Developers can build a modern facility tailored to meet market demand while keeping staff and maintenance costs low. These state-of-the-art stores can offer the full array of products and services demanded by today's customers.

On the other hand, developing can also be a disaster, especially for those who don't do their homework. We hear stories every day about people who built great looking facilities before they checked with the city and discovered that another developer had been given approval to build right down the street.

Worse, we've seen markets where several developers fail to do their homework. Without consulting the city's planning department, they all build in the same market and then try to open at the same time.

These developers have created far too much supply for their local market. This over-supply prevents them from leasing up in a timely fashion or at posted rates. Renters who sign up and move in do so only after negotiating huge discounts. Many of these developers may fail to lease up in time to pay off their loan. As a result, they either end up selling their facilities at a loss or losing them to the bank.

This isn't just bad for the individual developers. It's also tough on the existing self-storage owners who will lose tenants to the glut of cheap competition as they struggle to survive in an overbuilt market.

Sadly, this overbuilding has become common in many suburbs and newly-planned communities. Someone will say, "Hey, there are lots of people moving in so they will need storage." The problem arises when several developers have the same great idea, skip their homework, and rush into building at the same time.

There are also differences in the vital area of financing. Today, it's relatively easy to get a loan to buy an existing self-storage facility. This is because the store has an operating history that the bank can evaluate. If the bank likes the numbers it will usually make a loan on the business. Note, however, that first timers will probably be required to hire a self-storage property management company to run the property. Best of all, the lender will offer a loan that is fully non-recourse. This means that the buyer will not have to pledge assets. If a loan repayment problem emerges, the lender will simply take back the property.

On the other hand, it's much more difficult to get a loan to build a self-storage facility, especially for a first-timer without experience in self-storage or a successful track record in real estate. When banks do lend money for development projects they often insist on full recourse loans. This means that someone has to personally guarantee the loan with their own cash, personally held real estate, stocks, bonds, retirement accounts, precious works of art, and so forth. That individual's assets will be at risk if problems arise with the loan payments.

In summary, buying an existing self-storage facility is often a less risky choice than building from scratch. However, developing offers the higher profit potential. You could create a huge windfall; but you could also wind up bankrupt. The key to success is aligning yourself with the right people and doing your homework before making any decisions.

In addition to its higher risk profile, development in today's economic climate has been made very challenging by several factors including:

- High Land Prices, Requiring More Capital

When it comes to building new facilities, increases in land prices are pushing the "cost of entry" higher and higher. This impacts every stage of development by increasing the chances of failure.

- Increased Competition for Good Sites

As storage facilities move closer and closer to Main Street, self-storage developers find themselves competing with office, retail, multi-family, and mixed-use developers for the same locations.

- Long Lead Time to Profitability

A new self-storage facility will typically lease up at an average rate of 1,000 to 2,500 square feet per month. Thus, these facilities usually take longer to reach full occupancy than apartment buildings and other property types.

- Rising Building Materials Costs

Increased global demand for building materials such as concrete, lumber, and metal has created shortages in the United States. These shortages have lead to significant increases in material costs.

The result in many cases has been that developers who put together a budget and raise money will then find out that by the time they break ground, increased costs for building materials have turned their project upside down. Therefore, it is very important for developers to build enough of a contingency cushion into their models to protect them against fluctuations in materials and other costs.

- Look and Feel

This refers to a division of local government often called the Architectural Review Board (or a similar title). This board is charged with ensuring that new development blends into the existing community. It is concerned with setting and maintaining high standards. Often, this board tends to favor retail construction over new self-storage facilities. Self-storage facilities are typically seen in an unfavorable light because, as noted earlier, unlike retail stores, most do not generate significant sales tax revenue, and many areas do not have rental taxes.

Cities are increasingly demanding that self-storage facilities look and feel more like other structures in the community. In some areas, this means that it's no longer possible to build an inexpensive structure. City sanctions will force you to build using more costly guidelines, which could, for example, prohibit metal buildings or outdoor storage.

On the plus side, developers with deep pockets can follow these guidelines and build beautiful structures. These state-of-the-art stores hide storage units inside the building where they cannot be seen from the street. They often look more like trophy office buildings and ritzy hotels than self-storage facilities.

- Availability of Infrastructure Capacity

Many developers looking for a site find an abundance of locations that appear at first glance to work for their development. This is often because their real estate agents do not have the means to access infrastructure information during the due diligence process. Infrastructure factors can be crucial to the approval of the project. Important elements to consider are the availability and location of schools, the overcrowding of roads, and the capacity of the water and sewer system. This information should be presented to the developer early in the process.

- Complicated Zoning and Building Permit Issues

Often referred to as "entitlement uncertainty," this topic deals with the many procedures that must be followed in order to get permission to use the land for your intended purpose. In many cases we have seen developers work successfully with municipalities to change zoning in a way that allows self-storage development. However, this is often a difficult and expensive process.

In the old days when self-storage facilities were hidden away in industrial areas, zoning commissions tended to ignore them. There was little governmental oversight over a facility's appearance or impact on the community. But times have changed. Now that self-storage facilities are being built on Main Street, local authorities have become extremely interested in these developments.

Today, zoning compliance and building permits are crucial elements in any development. Here are some steps you can take to ensure that your Land Use Applications gain approval from local government authorities.

- Conform to the Local Government's Comprehensive Land Use Plan and Create Ways to Benefit the Local Community

The most basic element of this step is to follow the specific zoning and subdivision ordinances in question. It helps to remember that many local governments are now forming regional boards to oversee and assess regional development. The comprehensive plans they come up with have far-reaching implications if not followed, including the loss of federal funding. Many times, applicants are unaware that they must conform to these plans along with strict local ordinances.

- Consider the Benefit of the Proposed Use to the Local Government

Self-storage has a well-deserved reputation as a good civic citizen, yet many cities are reluctant to approve storage projects because they don't create tax revenues. This is a big issue in our industry and it's becoming more and more important as self-storage facilities move closer to Main Street.

These days, cities take a hard look at the benefits self-storage businesses will bring compared to industrial, commercial, and retail projects that all generate tax revenue. We've seen developers carefully plan a project and raise the money only to have the development stall out at the entitlement phase. The main problem is usually a simple one: Dealing with the city takes much longer than these developers had expected. Instead of waiting six to 12 months, developers are stalled for two to four years in many cases. Whenever a project is held up, funds are wasted. This can become very costly. In some cases, investors have lost enormous sums of money and even entire projects over entitlement issues.

Making a list of the numerous benefits the project brings to the community can be very helpful when dealing with city authorities. For example, every city wants more retail development because it brings greater sales tax revenue so be sure that your list includes tax revenues from the sale of miscellaneous products.

- Minimize the Potential for Citizen Opposition

Neighbors near a new development often organize in opposition of the proposed land use. The oft-heard statement at public hearings is, "We want this property to remain open space." These protests can affect the project approval, and sometimes, the approval board requests modification to the project, which costs the developer redesign fees. One never knows if a neighbor who opposes land use is a neighbor of a city council member. The first step for the developer and his team should be to identify the political "hot buttons" in the community that may impact decisions. Success may depend on the design team's ability to assess and respond to community issues.

- Manage the Approval Process

An appropriate team of qualified support people is critical, especially in the fields of real estate law, land planning, engineering design, and architecture. Thoughtful preparation in all four of these areas will enable applicants to be ready for challenges posed in obtaining timely approvals which will translate into more economically successful projects.

Without question the successful developers are those that are well prepared early in the development process. The destiny of development is in the hands of the public and the governing board. It's important that the applicant has a team in place that can emphasize the changes and concessions made to the plans to accommodate local agencies, neighborhood interests, and planning boards, while explaining the positive aspects of the development. This team must be skilled in responding to challenging questions during the process, and be able to anticipate which questions and concerns will be raised. This is a key factor in managing the land use approval process.

In summary, these challenges to development constitute considerable barriers to entry into the self-storage building business. However, this is not always a bad thing.

The good news is that some self-storage entrepreneurs have learned how to take advantage of markets with significant barriers to entrance. They deliberately seek out areas where development is more expensive and complicated. These developers know that "difficult" areas tend to have fewer facilities, lower saturation and higher demand. They want stringent building codes. They know that these restrictions will make it harder for someone else to open up next to them and reduce demand for their units. In other words, they see opportunity where others see only problems. In the right markets, these developers are enjoying high rental rates and occupancy.

On the bright side, there are still ample opportunities for developers. Good projects that are well located within a normal competitive arena can still provide strong returns.

How to Conduct a Proper Feasibility Study

Before committing to developing a self-storage facility, you need to conduct a thorough feasibility study. Like due diligence, feasibility studies will help you decide whether or not to move forward with your investment plan. The difference is that due diligence studies are conducted before buying, while feasibility studies are undertaken before building begins.

Feasibility studies are just as important as the due diligence process. These studies help you understand the feasibility or likelihood of your project being a success, and will help you determine whether or not to move forward with the development. It will also provide valuable information about what it will take to make the project profitable.

This is where you make or break your project. The problem is that most people try to skip steps. They may be trying to save a few bucks or they may be in the mood to rely on their instincts. These are usually the projects that go bust and are sold off at discount prices. To be successful, you must complete every single step of the process without cutting corners.

This guide to the feasibility study process will help you to decide when to spend money on a feasibility study, who to use and what you should expect. It's important to note that most feasibility studies are preceded by a market study, and that a facility's specific location must be determined prior to beginning a study.

Feasibility studies involve three main steps:

• Hiring a seasoned self-storage feasibility expert

- Examining this expert's findings with an open mind (never fall in love with a project before it's been analyzed in depth)

- Acting on the feasibility study's recommendations

Let's start with perhaps the most important question with any feasibility study.

- Where Do I Find A Good Consultant?

Cast a wide net in your search for a good consultant. Remember that just because people have been successful in industrial or retail real estate does not necessarily qualify them as experts in self-storage. You'll need to do your homework and check into backgrounds and experience.

Above all, be sure to find someone with extensive experience in successful self-storage projects. Many of those in the business are simply not that good at the work.

Here are some ways of finding the right consultant:

~ Referrals

Referrals are great, but if you're referred by colleagues who just thought they got a good report, then you are not moving forward! One good approach is to seek out successful projects and ask their owners for referrals.

Ask these owners, "Would you contact the same consultant for your next feasibility study? Were you in any way unhappy with the report?" Note that owners will probably be more open with you if you make it clear that you don't plan to compete in their markets.

Don't rule out a good referral just because he or she is based out of state. Distance is rarely an impediment. Most feasibility study experts are available to travel.

~ Magazine Ads

Trade magazines such as the *Mini-Storage Messenger* and *Inside Self-Storage* run ads offering feasibility studies. If a consultant does not advertise, he or she may be a low budget operator.

~ Trade Shows

Go to booths, speak with participating firms, and "kick the tires." A good firm will be highly visible and delighted to answer questions. A trade show is a major financial commitment on the part of an exhibitor. On average, it costs a company about $5,000 per trade show, considering travel and materials. Consultants who aren't willing to invest in meeting qualified prospects should raise questions: What are they hiding? Why do they keep such a low profile?

~ Educational Seminars

This is a good way to learn more about the process (unless the session is an "infomercial" aimed more at marketing than education). You may be able to gain some keen insight as to the quality of the consultant by the lengths to which they will go to help you become a better, more informed consumer.

~ Trade Associations

Deal only with consultants who are members of the Self Storage Association, and preferably those who are active in the association. Giving back to the industry is an important part of the process. Look for a consultant who is active in both state and national associations.

~ The Internet

When you're searching on the Web, take each potential consultant's Web site for a thorough test drive.

Ask yourself:
- How good is the firm's Web site?
- Can I view reports on-line?
- Are there any samples of their work?
- Are their prices posted?
- Do they describe the various levels of service they offer?
- Are consultants' resumes posted?
- What kind of information are they willing to share?

Once you've narrowed down your search, ask potential candidates the following questions:

~ How long have you been in the self-storage business?
~ What is the depth of your experience with self-storage?
~ Do you own your own self-storage facility?
~ If not, why not?
~ Can you give me a list of the projects you've worked on?

~ Which markets do you have the most experience with?
~ What are your most successful projects?
~ Why did they turn out so well?
~ What are your biggest project failures?
~ Why did things go wrong?
~ Can you give me a list of references?
~ Do you carry professional liability insurance?

• What should the feasibility study report include?

Subject to the purpose of the report, the report should contain the following essential elements:

~ Table of Contents
~ Self-Storage Industry Data
~ Area, Location, and Competition Map
~ Project Description
~ Property Photographs
~ Community Data
~ Municipality Data
~ Flood Map
~ Macro and Micro Site Analysis
~ Square Foot Per Capita Analysis
~ Market Demand
~ Definition and Comment on Primary and Secondary Market
~ Competitive Analysis: Primary and Market
~ Project Site Layout
~ Unit and Space Layout
~ Unit Mix and Rental Rates
~ Absorption Analysis
~ Exit Strategy
~ Store Operations Commentary
~ Insurance Quote
~ Yellow Page Quote
~ Construction Cost Estimates
~ Five to Seven Years Month-by-Month Budgets
~ Investment Return Analysis
~ Conclusion and Recommendations

See Appendix E for a copy of a Sample Feasibility Checklist.

CHOOSING THE RIGHT SITE LAYOUT AND UNIT MIX

Site Layout - Site layout refers to a project's ground map. In most cases, the owner works with a local architect or civil engineer familiar with self-storage and local zoning regulations. The goal is to develop a ground map that maximizes the size and shapes of the buildings without violating regulations regarding items such as setbacks, drainage, and fire lanes.

Basic choices include:

- Single or multistory

- Drive-up storage units or park and walk in

Once the legislative restrictions have been mapped out, the challenge is relatively easy to visualize. Simply imagine that you are a first-time visitor to the proposed facility. What is the most convenient way for you to enter the site and park? What's the best route for getting your belongings inside the building, onto an elevator and into your unit? You and your local expert must adjust the buildings and their shapes on the site layout until all customers can reach their units with the greatest possible ease.

Like customer access, vehicle access is also an important element in site layout. It's essential for example, to provide wide aisles so large vehicles can enter and unload with ease. Check with the local fire department for up-to-date requirements regarding hydrant placement and the fire truck's turning radius.

Unit Mix - As noted earlier, unit mix refers to the variety of different sized storage areas offered. Getting the unit mix right means understanding the customers who will be using that storage. Business customers for example, will prefer larger units while college students rent much smaller spaces. Get this ratio wrong and the result will be an under-rented facility.

Some self-storage facilities are built with metal partitions dividing the units. These walls can be moved to adjust the unit mix. However, not all problems regarding unit mix can be resolved so easily. Indeed, major mistakes in this area can sink the entire development. Big mistakes can occur for example, in the area of specialty storage. There is little point in building climate-controlled wine storage units in a market area where no potential customers exist.

The problem is that once construction has finished, it's often difficult to adjust the unit mix to meet inaccurate projections or changing markets. What if you have a small average unit size but your target market is losing renter-occupied housing? The newcomers are homeowners. Unlike apartment renters, those who own their own homes prefer to rent large units. If you're unable to adjust your average unit size upward, those potential customers will look elsewhere.

Whenever possible, the unit mix should be tailored to your site and market.

BASIC DEVELOPMENT COSTS/LEASE UP/BREAK-EVEN OCCUPANCY

The goal here is to begin covering development costs as quickly as possible by having tenants ready to move in as soon as the facility is complete.

Development costs include such items as:

- Startup costs

- Land

- Entitlement

- Feasibility reports

- Architecture and design

- Construction and materials

- Marketing and lease up

As a general rule of thumb, consider that a self-storage facility could have been built for $30 to $60 per square foot (excluding land costs) in 2004.

Conversion projects will cost much less. Here development costs can be as low as $15 to $25 per square foot (excluding land costs). Note however, that conversions are often plagued by cost overruns. Unexpected problems, such as internal walls that cannot be moved, often arise during the conversion process.

RV and boat storage facilities typically incur similar development costs. All-in costs range between $15 to $25 per square foot for the average RV and boat storage project (excluding land costs).

Lease Up - Lease up (or absorption) refers to the period of time needed to fill your project with renters. In commercial and retail projects, lease up can happen relatively quickly. Before financing is approved for these property types, one large customer must typically be secured. Often times, this "single large customer" will rent all the available space and sign a long-term contract.

A few years ago, the average self-storage facility leased up in approximately 18 to 24 months. With today's increased building activity and intense competition, lease up now takes many facilities 36 to 48 months. Big facilities will usually take longer than small facilities to reach full occupancy.

An effective lease-up strategy is essential in order to achieve the fastest possible lease up. The aim is to get 85 to 90 percent of the units rented as quickly as possible at the best possible rents while still retaining customers.

Amongst other items, an effective lease-up strategy involves:

- Customer service

- Pricing

- Incentive

- Discounts

Break-Even Occupancy - In the industry's early days, the break-even occupancy point for storage was much lower than that of other property types. A typical facility could reach break-even at 55- to 65-percent occupancy. In recent years, higher land and building costs have brought the self-storage break-even point closer to those of retail, industrial and housing.

When it comes to matters of occupancy, experienced owners often prefer to run at 90-percent capacity. The reason they chose not to operate at 100 percent is that they never want to put themselves in a position where they have no product to rent to new customers.

Over the years we have seen several instances where a landlord chooses to operate at 100-percent occupancy, and gets a reputation in the community for never having any space to rent. Eventually, customers move out of the storage facility and need to be replaced. Unfortunately, the landlord's reputation has created a situation where there is very little new customer traffic. Often, these stores run into very high vacancy issues down the road.

To avoid this problem, experienced self-storage operators choose to run their facilities at 90-percent occupancy. Whenever occupancy levels exceed 90 percent, these owners raise rates, forcing some people to move into cheaper storage. Eventually, new customers come in to take their place and all the tenants end up paying the new higher rates.

FINANCING YOUR DEVELOPMENT PROJECT

If your feasibility study is positive, you can plan to proceed with the development process. The next step is to arrange financing. We cover the steps involved in obtaining the best possible financing package later in this book.

CHAPTER EIGHT

How to Acquire a Self-Storage Facility

There are two ways to get into the self-storage business. We've already discussed the idea of developing your own self-storage facility. In this chapter we'll examine approaches to buying into the business.

The Advantages of Buying vs. Building

If you read the last chapter on building your own self-storage facility and you still don't know if you want to build or buy then it's a safe bet that building is not the right thing for you. It's time to consider the second way to get into the business: the acquisition of an existing facility.

There are several advantages to buying rather than building your first self-storage facility. These advantages include:

* Speed to Market

Buying an existing operation will get you into the business faster. You can avoid the entire development process which typically takes several months, if not years.

* Predictability

The development process is not only lengthy, it is also fraught with inherent risks. These include the uncertainties of renting up, building an inappropriate site layout and/or unit mix, and changes in local supply and demand before the project is completed. Buying a self-storage facility gives you a solid track record based on an established operating history (assuming that you conduct thorough due diligence so that you know what you're buying).

* Easy Financing

Purchasers of self-storage facilities can choose from a wide variety of loans from multiple sources. Self-storage facilities can be bought with non-recourse loans that are much easier to finance. One of the main reasons development projects fail is because qualified investors are often reluctant to sign on as loan guarantors.

Today's historically low interest rates would make acquisition a relatively simple choice if more facilities were on the market. In fact, few quality projects are for sale, even at the higher prices available to potential sellers as a result of low interest rates. Those owners who may be contemplating a sale usually prefer to approach institutional buyers on a principal-to-principal basis.

As you are probably not an institutional buyer, you'll have to find a seller the old-fashioned way. You're going to have to do your homework.

WHERE CAN I FIND SELF-STORAGE BUSINESSES FOR SALE?

With all of the advantages self-storage facilities offer, it's not surprising that self-storage has become a very "hot" property type. Today's market is further constricted by shortfalls in the supply of available properties. There simply aren't that many properties for sale, especially in comparison to other property types like industrial, commercial, multi-family, and single-tenant housing.

In short, today's increasingly competitive environment can be tough on those looking to buy self-storage facilities. Newcomers are jumping into an existing pool of buyers eager to take advantage of low interest rates and the self-storage industry's bright future.

So, Where Do You Find Good Facilities For Sale?

The best approach is to employ a combination of resources in your search for the right property. These sources include:

- Hiring a real estate broker who specializes in self-storage properties

- Consulting industry-specific listing services

- Cold calling existing owners and operators on the telephone

- Expending good old fashioned shoe leather by visiting sites and talking to owners

The first two items on this list are pretty self-explanatory. Let's examine the final two in more detail. Both of these approaches involve efforts to find an owner with a quality store who is interested in selling. The problem is that many of the properties on the market have already been picked over by discriminating buyers, and the remnants will often be less than ideal for your purposes. The best way around this problem is to find a property before it hits the market.

Where should you look for this property? To answer this question, let's briefly examine the reasons owners decide to sell profitable self-storage facilities:

- Death

Usually the demise of an owner triggers taxes that have to be paid relatively quickly. Sometimes a facility will be sold to meet these tax demands.

- Divorce

As with death, divorce can lead to the forced sale of a self-storage facility.

- Partnership Break-Ups

Often the only clean break involves selling the store.

- Bankruptcy

Some owners may for example, borrow against their self-storage facility in order to buy other riskier investments. When these fail, their facilities are often sold to cover their debts.

- The Timing/Price is Right

You may find an owner who has simply decided that this is the right time to take advantage of market conditions. He or she may be simply ready to retire or hoping to sell at what they perceive to be the top of the local market.

If you can build a strong social and business network in your target community, you may be able to find one of these situations.

What happens then? If you find a property you like, you'll need to make an offer on that property. Then it's time to exercise some patience. As you do so, remember this familiar rule of thumb in real estate: For every 100 properties you consider, you will probably make 10 offers. If you're lucky two or three of these may result in counteroffers. If you're even luckier, one of your offers will be accepted.

The danger is of course, that as capital pours in and cap rates continue to fall, frustrated buyers are tempted to place riskier bets on lower-quality stores. This temptation must be resisted at all costs. It's far better to demonstrate discipline than to rush into a dubious deal. Remember, in real estate you make your money on the buy.

A seller's market drives buyers back to the basics. Today, more than ever, finding the right deal depends on doing your homework in an objective and dispassionate way. Sure, it's exciting when you finally find a property that you like and begin framing an offer. But this isn't the time to let your judgment be clouded by a desire to close a deal.

Instead, with your enthusiasm tightly leashed, maintain a laser-sharp focus on the fundamentals:

- The facility's current income

- Your estimated operating costs

Then add up the following costs:

- The seller's asking price

- Closing costs and fees

- Curing deferred maintenance

- Necessary improvements

- Managing the investment

- Financing

- Providing returns to your investors

- Cost of ownership

- Cash reserves

Evaluate these expenses closely. As you do so ask yourself questions such as:

- Is your offer enough to make the deal work?

- Has your offer left you enough room, after factoring in all your costs, to get the kind of return you need?

- Have you added a cushion so that you can continue paying back your investors during difficult times?

Remember to be patient and unemotional. Avoid falling in love with any one property, no matter how well it may seem to fit your search image. When emotions become involved, the risks go far beyond paying more than a facility is worth. They include such mistakes as purchasing a property with serious, even fundamental flaws or rushing into a market that has already been overbuilt. In both cases you will, at the very least, have overpaid for your self-storage facility.

How Do I Value an Existing Self-Storage Asset?

Before you can make an offer on a self-storage facility you must determine its value. There are many factors involved in valuing self-storage properties, including:

- Features and Benefits

First and foremost you must visit and tour the property. Inspect your proposed purchase in great detail. Develop an accurate picture of its features and benefits (See Appendix F for a Sample Facility Walk-Through Report).

- Capitalization Rates

A capitalization rate or cap rate is defined as the expected annual return on a real estate investment. A cap rate of 10 for example, suggests that the buyer can expect an annual return of 10 percent.

Because they are based on income streams, cap rates can help investors establish values both within and between different real estate property types. Property value is calculated by dividing the property's net operating income (NOI) by the cap rate.

In this example, the Seaside self-storage facility is generating a net operating income of $200,000 per year. Cap rates in Seaside for self-storage properties are currently 10 percent.

Using these figures, we can calculate the Seaside self-storage facility's property value using the following formula:

Property Value = NOI/Cap Rate.

So Property Value = $200,000/0.10 = $2,000,000

Using the same example, we could calculate the Cap Rate based on the NOI and the seller's asking price, as follows:

Cap Rate = NOI/Estimated Value

So Cap Rate = $200,000/$2,000,000 = 0.10

Viewed over time, cap rates provide a good indicator of the overall marketplace. Cap rates fluctuate because they tend to follow changes in interest rates.

As interest rates fall, property prices tend to rise, lowering cap rates. For example, in 2000, the average cap rate for a self-storage facility in the United States was approximately 10 percent. By 2004, interest rates had fallen significantly, and as a result, the average cap rate for a self-storage facility had fallen to 7.62 percent.

The idea of how cap rates work can be confusing to real estate newcomers. Just remember, as cap rates fall, property prices will rise, and vice-versa.

- Your Numbers vs. Their Numbers – Actual vs. Proforma

When viewing income statements, it's important to distinguish between proforma (projected numbers) and the actual figures.

Actual numbers reflect what is actually occurring or has occurred at the facility. Proforma numbers are projected figures based on an estimate of what "could happen". Be very wary about committing to a deal based on the seller's proforma. If sellers were really so sure about things like the ability to increase income or decrease expenses, they probably would have already done so themselves.

Unfortunately, these days many properties are listed using a cap rate based on proforma figures. As noted above, proforma figures represent the seller or broker's best guess or projection regarding how the property might perform in the future. Remember that this approach can be used to artificially inflate a facility's numbers so that they look better. In some cases, these figures may not, in any way, reflect how the facility is actually performing.

All too often, buyers neglect this simple precaution. They enter into deals based on inflated proforma cap rates and run into problems. Consider for example, a seller who puts a property up for sale and advertises a price based on a 10-percent cap rate. Based on this information, the buyer believes that the facility is generating a 10-percent return.

During due diligence the buyer discovers that the facility is only 50 percent occupied and that its rental rates are 50 percent under market. Instead of pricing the deal accurately, the seller (or perhaps the broker involved) based the price on a projection of potential future earnings if the facility was 100 percent rented at above-market rates. Beware of this all-too-common situation. Your best protection lies in asking the right questions before taking any action.

- Physical vs. Economic Occupancy

One way to avoid such problems is by clearly distinguishing between the physical and economic occupancy of the self-storage facility in question. This important distinction can have a huge impact on the amount of income actually generated.

As previously mentioned, physical occupancy refers to the number of units or square feet rented, without regard to rates. Economic occupancy is a more accurate metric. It measures the rents that these units are actually generating, factoring in all discounts and incentives.

The safest approach is to never rely on figures provided by the seller. Review all the numbers you can get your hands on in exhaustive detail. Question everything. If for example, the seller assures you that you'll be able to raise rents without difficulty, ask one simple question, "If that's so, why haven't you already raised your rents?"

It can sometimes be difficult to get at the actual figures. Smaller facilities don't always have sophisticated accounting software. It is however, always worth the effort to obtain accurate figures. If a seller insists that he or she keeps their records "on the back of an envelope" take this as a warning sign.

- Property Tax Increases Triggered by the Property's Purchase

As most homeowners know only too well, property taxes are often one of the biggest expenses involved in owning real estate. These levies are often made worse by the addition of several local taxes, with such creative names as parcel tax, along with charges for the debt service on any bonds approved by popular vote, and so on. The net result of all this is that, in most parts of the country, property owners are paying fairly hefty tax bills.

When evaluating a facility's numbers, be sure to use the new property tax that will be levied rather than the lesser amount the current owner is paying. There is often a significant difference, especially if you're considering older facilities or new developments.

Imagine, for example, that you are considering buying a 30-year-old self-storage facility from its original owner-builder. When first built, this facility was assessed at a fair market value of $10,000. The seller has been paying the state of California property taxes based on that $10,000 for the last 30 years. California's Proposition 13 limits the general property tax rate to one percent of the assessed value. For simplicity's sake, we'll assume that there haven't been any additions to this tax. Our seller will therefore list his annual property tax, quite accurately as one percent of $10,000, or $100.

He was asking $2,100,000 for his store, but you've bargained him down to an even $2,000,000. You will be taxed one percent of this new assessed value. As the new owner, you will be paying $20,000, not $100 in property taxes.

- Salaries

As is the case with most numbers provided by the seller, salary figures can mislead the unwary buyer. Review all salary figures carefully. You may discover for example, that the owner/operator has never drawn a salary, thus creating a payroll savings that you will be unable to duplicate.

- *Yellow Pages*

is another example of an area where the seller's figures may not give you a complete picture of the property you are considering buying. In certain markets, *Yellow Page* ads can be very expensive. Check that this expense is reflected accurately in the figures. Additionally, make sure that the facility under consideration has paid for its current *Yellow Pages* advertising in full. Some sellers will have prepaid only a portion of their bill. The second and often considerably larger payment will become an unexpected expense for you down the road.

It's also a good idea to check that the ad hasn't been cancelled. In some instances, sellers, knowing that they are selling out, have been known to call and cancel their ads. Since the ad is still in the book, you may not realize that you have lost this crucial advertising until the publication deadline has passed.

- Deferred Maintenance

Another trap for the unwary buyer can be found in the area of deferred maintenance. Don't ignore the future impact of maintenance problems, such as outdated roofs and broken doors. Sooner or later, these items will have to be rectified, reducing your returns.

Clearly, those searching for the right store need all the patience they can muster. As you push ahead with your search, it may help to remember the ancient adage *caveat emptor*—let the buyer beware. In many cases, the best deals are the deals you walk away from without ever writing a check. At the very least, you'll be avoiding "buyer's remorse."

Congratulations! You've persevered with your search and finally located a property that meets your criteria. You've even made an offer. While the seller is reviewing this offer, use the time to begin preparing your Purchase and Sales Agreement. (See Appendix G for a list of items to include in this agreement.)

Once you and the seller have agreed on a price, entering into a process of rigorous due diligence will help you make that all-important final purchase decision.

HOW TO CONDUCT THOROUGH DUE DILIGENCE ON YOUR ACQUISITION TARGET.

Due Diligence is the essence of any good real estate transaction. This process is defined as the act of carefully reviewing, checking and verifying all of the facts and issues involved in a real estate transaction before proceeding with that deal. In lending it is, among other things, verification of employment, income and savings; review of the appraisal, credit report, and status of the title. In practice, this often involves a cat-and-mouse game played between buyers and sellers, and lenders and borrowers, that seeks to identify the risks of the pending transaction.

Due diligence means different things to different people. It's not an appraisal process. The result isn't intended to establish a value, although that may well be a byproduct of the process. The goal is to find facts and disclose risks, rather than offer an opinion as to whether the prospective buyer can provide the solutions.

Newcomers are often surprised when one of the first risks to be identified is their own lack of experience. This disclosure is typically couched in the following terms: "If you've never owned and operated a self-storage property, what makes you think you are qualified to sustain the profitable operations of a smoothly operating property, never mind turn-around a distressed property?"

As newcomers struggle to answer this tough question, they can be forgiven for thinking of the due diligence process as a deal-killer. Yet, in many cases, due diligence can help close the deal.

Here is a short list of how a rigorous due diligence process conducted by professional, knowledgeable self-storage experts can enhance a transaction:

- Discovery of hidden income; improving the deal

- Discovery of potential income; providing upside to the transaction

- Disclosure of expense savings missed by the current owner

- In "grooming" the detailed general ledger, the due diligence expert may find expenses that should have been capitalized

- Uncovering one-time expenses that do not influence year-to-year normal operations

- Finding incorrect figures that incorrectly inflated the figures

- Discovering facts that make the market more attractive than in the past

As this list makes clear, the due diligence process is not one that you would ever want to conduct on your own. You may be a good owner-operator, but that does not necessarily mean that you are a good buyer of real estate. There is a very big difference.

First and foremost comes one simple fact: The time to conduct due diligence is before you sign on the bottom line! Once you buy the property, it's too late for second thoughts, also known as buyer's remorse. Novices to this business should always seek expert counsel before putting hundreds of thousands, or millions of dollars at risk.

As we saw in our earlier examples of *Yellow Page* ads and missing management salaries, there are many traps waiting for unwary buyers. With that in mind, let's look at two situations in which the due diligence process could have avoided potentially tragic results.

In the first situation the purchaser didn't conduct a thorough due diligence effort before he purchased a property for cash. When he sought financing, his lender performed due diligence and found that the purchaser had been "duped" by the seller. The property was not generating the income indicated by the seller's data. In fact, the actual performance of the property was 75 percent less than claimed.

This buyer made two major mistakes. His first was ignoring due diligence. The second was that he didn't ask himself the following question before buying the property: Why has this property not been sold to one of the major buyers of self-storage properties?

The second situation was a little less traumatic. The purchaser engaged a firm to conduct due diligence after he closed. He discovered that there was a moratorium on building or expanding his property (and one of his reasons for purchasing was to expand). He also found out that a new 80,000-square-foot, state-of-the-art property had been approved nearby and permits were ready to be issued. So, not only could he not build if he wanted, he had a first generation product in a market with a proposed state-of-the-art property ready to go to market. As you can imagine, this purchaser wished that he had performed due diligence before he closed.

There are numerous buyers of self-storage properties ready, willing and able to close on self-storage transactions. If the property you're considering is the correct size and price; located properly; and in a good market, chances are you will never get a chance to buy that facility. It will be sold before it ever reaches the market. Note that in all but a very small number of situations this store will be purchased by an institution.

In many cases, property that is available on the open market will have problems. If you buy such a property, keep in mind that those problems become your problems. Also note that such a property may well be easier to buy than to sell. This may be due to several factors:

- The same negatives that prevented the institutions from buying it before will likely still be around to haunt you in the sales process.

- Lenders may have the same problems with the property as the major buyers of self-storage. In order to get financing, buyers may have to find a lender who doesn't know enough about the property or industry to make a good lending decision!

With this in mind, approach all prospective purchases with a healthy dose of skepticism and ask yourself these questions:

- Why is the owner selling?
- Why hasn't a REIT, institution, or sophisticated self-storage operator bought this self-storage facility?
- Why aren't the professionals showing this property interested in buying it (assuming that they're self-storage owners, brokers, or industry insiders)?

Build on this healthy level of skepticism by making yourself a promise. Promise that you'll never close on a property until you have conducted a thorough due diligence effort. Unless due diligence is your core business, hire a professional for this task. Don't risk making this large purchase without the right kind of assistance.

The best way to get this help is by building a team of professionals. Here's a list of the people you need on your due diligence team along with their responsibilities:

- An Attorney

Among Other Things, Your Attorney Should Review These Legal Documents:

~ Purchase and Sale Agreement
~ Entity Documents:
  o Does the seller have the right to sell the property?
  o Are there partnership issues?
~ Title Insurance Binder
~ Non-compete clauses
~ Zoning Compliance
~ Ability to Replace Improvements as grandfathered (non-compliant sites)
~ Environmental Reports (particularly if there are issues)
~ How pro-rations are handled at close
~ How receivables are handled at close
~ When does the close technically take place:
  o On the day of escrow?
  o When funds are sent?
  o When funds are received?
  o When deeds are filed?
~ Personal property purchase agreement
~ Trade Name and D/B/A documentation and rights
~ Issue and opinion letter on lease document
~ Reps and Warrantees

- An Accountant

Preferably a Certified Public Accountant (or storage consultant) should be checking:

~ Bank statements compared to financial statements
~ Cash to accrual basis conversion
~ Accounts receivable and accounts payable reports
~ Reconciliation of site management reports to the documents originally

submitted for making the purchase decision
~ Physical inventory
~ Retail sales inventory

• Self-Storage Due Diligence Expert

A self-storage due diligence expert should do the following:

~ Audit lease documents
~ Conduct verbal estoppels
~ Market evaluation
~ Examine the propensity for rental rate improvements
~ Interview and assess on-site personnel
~ Interview and retain or hire third-party management company
~ Prepare three years budgets
~ Examine manager and employee incentive program
~ Evaluate retail sales program
~ Software evaluation
~ Archive integrity
~ Make operational suggestions to enhance the property
~ Inform you of ways to reduce operating expenses
~ Examine and comment on existing management practices

• Title Insurance Agent

A title insurance agent should check survey liabilities, including:

~ Easements
  ○ A right of way giving persons other than the owner access to or over a property.
~ Encroachments
  ○ An improvement, structure, or part of a structure that intrudes illegally on another's property.
~ Setback violations
  ○ The distance required from a boundary line that can not be built within.
~ Ownership issues
  ○ Who has proper title to a property, or a vested interest.
~ Pending litigation
  ○ Law suits that could affect title (also known as *lis pendins*).
~ General title flaws
  ○ Issues of a general nature that cause title not to be marketable or insurable.

~ Construction or contractor liens
  o Unpaid or unreleased obligations that create a lien or security interest on or against the property.

- Environmental Consultant

An environmental consultant will provide the following:

~ Phase I Environmental Site Assessment (ESA)
  o This is an important action a purchaser can take to learn about the property's past use, the environmental conditions at the site and adjoining sites, and the likely presence of hazardous substances.
~ Further testing as needed
  o Also known as a Phase II Assessment, this is when the consultant determines that they do not have enough information to make a decision and requireadditional testing.
~ No Further Action Letters
  o When the governing authority signs off on a property and issues a letter stating that no more testing or monitoring is necessary.
~ Indemnification Agreements
  o The person or persons who have caused contamination or an unacceptable environmental condition agrees to pay for the cleanup or reimburse a party for costs associated with the contamination.
~ "Bugs and Bunnies, Turtles and Owls"
  o When a property is affected by the presence of a protected species, with these four being the most common.
~ Wetland Delineation
  o The U.S. Corps of Engineers has determined that some land areas must be used to allow water to stand or percolate back into the water table. These areas are commonly called wetlands, and can be mitigated, but most often must be preserved by the developer.

- Engineer

An engineer will issue:

~ Property Condition Report
~ Structural Evaluation
~ Permit Compliance
~ Code Violation Exam
~ Life Safety Issues

- Surveyor

A surveyor can provide:

~ Boundary
  ○ A survey showing only the boundaries or property lines, this usually doesn't meet the scope required by a title company, financial institution, or prudent buyer.
~ "As-built"
  ○ After the project is completed, a survey is conducted and prepared to show the finished improvements.
- Insurance Agent

An insurance agent will discuss:

~ Current insurance coverage
~ Cost of new insurance

- Property Tax Consultant

A property tax consultant can predict:

~ Special tax considerations in the past that will expire
~ Future tax liabilities
~ The likelihood of appealing tax billings and winning

- Lender

Conducting thorough due diligence will serve two purposes:

~ It will help you determine if the information upon which you based your original offer is accurate.
~ It will give you advanced notice of information the lender will discover during due diligence.

What's more, the due diligence process will help you realize the complexities involved in judging a property's ability to generate and sustain income. This perspective will help you negotiate with lenders who tend to view properties more critically than their borrowers. It's their job to take an objective, macro view.

Among other things, lenders examine:

~ Demographics and their role in marketing
~ The strength and diversity of the local economy and employment market
~ Changes in occupancy and rental rates
~ The likely impact of competition and emerging competition

Many borrowers are reluctant to disclose the weaknesses of their property for fear of upsetting the deal. This is usually the result of emotional attachments to their sites. Avoid this shortsighted approach. Use your lender as a valuable sounding board for your investment choices. Clearly, the lender's opinion shouldn't be the only opinion you solicit before making your decision, but this source clearly merits serious consideration.

When a lender doesn't see the "upside" in a transaction, one of these three factors may be responsible:

~ You haven't properly documented the property's potential.
~ The lender doesn't understand self-storage lending and operations.
~ You are operating on your own instincts. If you really do have good instincts this approach may work for a while. It isn't, however, a strategy for success in the long run.

The bottom line: When the advantages of a real estate transaction are genuine, those advantages are relatively easily documented.

Lenders aren't born to be deal-killers. They are likely to be as disappointed as you are if a deal falls out because of discovery during due diligence. Lenders don't earn money from analyzing deals; they make money by making loans. You may have a lower threshold for risk than your lender.

Here is a simple formula to follow when working with lenders:

~ Identify the risk
~ Understand the causes
~ Mitigate the risk with solutions

Many lenders are turning to professional due diligence providers for expert assistance in identifying and analyzing the risks of a transaction. The due diligence process gives lenders a clear picture not just of valuation but also of cash flow and cash flow preservation. It also creates a detailed analysis of each asset's ability to perform in both expected and unexpected market and financial conditions. Most importantly, a complete due diligence report provides solutions to mitigate the potential concerns of a lender or rating agency.

There are several risk levels for a lender which due diligence should address:

~ What circumstances are likely to result in the borrower defaulting?
~ What is the likelihood that the borrower will default?
~ To whom and how will the bank sell the asset if they are required to foreclose?
~ How long will it take to sell the property?
~ How much can the bank expect to net out of the sale, and will it be enough to recover their principal, interest and costs?

The process of due diligence for the lender will aim to satisfy several criteria:

~ Does the transaction meet the bank's lending parameters?
~ Is the underwriting in conformity with bank policy?
~ Will the loan meet the requirements of the rating agencies?
~ Is the loan officer experienced enough in self-storage to recognize hidden risks?
~ What might a prospective purchaser during foreclosure find is wrong with the property?
~ To whom can the bank sell the loan if they don't wish to hold it in their portfolio?

Concentrating on the many issues revealed by a rigorous due diligence process will reveal your target property's ability to generate and sustain income. This objective perspective will be invaluable during negotiations with the seller and potential lenders. Best of all, it will help you meet your most important goal—protecting your investors.

See Appendix H for a Sample Due Diligence Checklist.

FINANCING YOUR ACQUISITION

If the due diligence process results in a green light for proceeding with your purchase, the next step is to arrange financing. We cover the steps involved in obtaining the best possible financing package in the next chapter.

CHAPTER NINE

How to Finance Your Facility

How Is Self-Storage Viewed by the Investment Community?

In recent years, self-storage has greatly improved its standing within the investment community. In fact, storage is viewed by many as one of today's best investments.

This newfound confidence in self-storage is reflected in the rich diversity of financing options available in today's capital markets. Owners seeking to buy self-storage facilities can choose between fixed-rate and floating-rate loans. Developers find construction and bridge financing readily available. Need to refinance? You'll be welcomed with open arms by lenders who are eager to provide financing for viable self-storage projects.

When it comes to getting a loan, today's financial markets offer a wide range of choices. However, leverage requirements are higher in self-storage than in other real estate investments. This discrepancy is due to three main factors:

- Longer Speed-To-Profit Cycle

As noted earlier in the chapter on development, self-storage facilities usually take longer to fully lease up than apartment buildings and other property types.

- Lack of Long-Term Leases

It is somewhat ironic that banks prefer to see long-term leases when month-to-month leases allow self-storage facility owners to improve profitability by raising rents on a regular basis.

- Self-Storage is an Operating Business

We're not just buying real estate; we're also buying the business that sits on top of that land. Because all businesses have the propensity to fail, banks and other lenders are predisposed to view them as risky investments. For this reason, banks require very thorough feasibility studies on developments and due diligence reports on acquisitions.

Like most real estate projects, buying or building a self-storage facility involves relatively large sums of money. As a result, self-storage transactions usually depend on loans secured by the real property.

The challenge is of course, to find the right loan for your specific situation. We'll briefly review the financing sources and options available in today's loan markets.

WHAT ARE THE MAJOR SOURCES OF CAPITAL?

Today's financial marketplace offers a wide range of potential lenders. Different lenders offer different kinds of loans and make different requirements of the borrower. It is important that you exercise care when selecting your lender and that you understand everything that is expected of you as a borrower.

This list of lenders that provide loans for self-storage properties includes:

• Banks

Banks are usually local, relationship-driven lenders. Most are portfolio lenders that are conservative and require a personal guarantee from the borrower. Banks typically provide short-term loans. They can be one of the most inexpensive sources of capital. Banks have fairly flexible pricing and terms, but they must adhere to strict regulation over third party reports and requirements. Examples of banks include Wells Fargo, Bank of America, and Imperial Capital Bank.

• Credit Companies

Typically a little higher priced than other types of lenders, the credit company is often the most flexible in customizing loans to meet borrowers' specific needs. Often bridge lenders, credit companies can be portfolio lenders or conduit lenders. With more complex loans, or less qualified borrowers, credit companies may require recourse (for at least a portion of the loan). Examples of credit companies are GE Capital and Westinghouse.

• Hard Money Lenders

Flexible, but very expensive, hard-money lenders are typically used for interim financing and for borrowers with credit problems. Typically known for quick closings (sometimes less than two weeks), the pricing is reflective of the level of risk. Loan-to-value ratios are often fairly conservative, in the 50- to 60-percent range. Expect a high interest rate and high points for the origination. Mercury Capital is an example of a hard-money lender.

• Investment Banks

Investment banks can function as interim lenders for large transactions. Their loans are almost always non-recourse with very strict underwriting requirements. Examples of investment banks include Bear Stern, Lehman Brothers, and Goldman-Sachs.

- Leasing Companies

A relatively new source of financing for self-storage projects, leasing companies can finance the purchase of buildings, construction, and equipment. Typically these lenders are interested in smaller transactions and are long-term financing propositions. High leverage and long-term loans are common characteristics of leasing companies. One example is Wells Fargo Leasing, formerly Telmark.

- Life Companies

Usually reserved for larger, high-quality projects ("A" properties in "A" markets), life insurance companies will offer some of the best rates at moderately conservative levels of leverage. They're sometimes very particular about the strengths of the borrower. Most life companies have fairly strict policies, and many don't understand self-storage projects. Mass Mutual and Prudential are examples of life insurance companies that lend money for self-storage properties.

- Loan or Mortgage Brokers

Flexible in assisting you in finding the best deal, or the one that best suits your needs, brokers are not usually lenders. Instead, they function as an intermediary working on your behalf. If the broker is an exclusive correspondent, a broker may be the only way to access a particular lender (most likely a life company). Borrowers are encouraged to work with brokers experienced in self-storage loans. The broker can assist you in packaging your loan for the best, most expedient presentation to lenders, but may or may not work with banks. Examples include Buchanan Storage Capital, Beacon Realty Capital, and Coast-To-Coast Storage.

- Private-Money Lenders

These are typically very, very flexible and very, very expensive sources of capital. Private-money lenders are usually considered as the last resort for capital (just behind hard-money lenders). Often unlicensed and without regulation, private-money lenders can be terrific sources for challenging transactions.

LOAN CLASSIFICATIONS

- Conduit Loan

Also known as a securitized loan, these loans are bundled or pooled together and sold to bondholders. Conduit loans provide better financing terms without a requirement for personal guarantees. Conduit loans funded over the past 10 years have the lowest default rate of all property types at .99 percent. This compares with a 4.51 percent average delinquency rate for all other property types including office, retail, industrial, hotels and multi-family.

Characteristics include:
~ Non recourse (no personal guarantees)
~ Significant prepayment penalties
~ Lock-outs (periods of time you can not prepay)
~ Inflexible documentation
~ Higher leverage
~ Strength of the property is the strength of the loan
~ Seek mature cash flow – strong prior operating history vs. proforma
~ Higher due diligence costs
~ Expensive to close

• Portfolio Loan

These loans aren't usually sold. Rather, they are held by the specific financial institution.

Characteristics Include:
~ Recourse (require personal guarantees)
~ Borrower is heavily weighted in the loan-granting process
~ Flexible
~ Often relationship-driven
~ Reduced due diligence costs
~ Lower closing costs and legal costs)

Today, many borrowers are turning to conduit loans over portfolio loans. Conduit loans provide better financing terms without a requirement for personal guarantees. The only drawback to conduit loans lies in their inflexibility; conduit loans can't be sold or refinanced.

SELF-STORAGE FINANCING OVERVIEW
As noted earlier, today's financial marketplace offers a wide range of potential lenders. Once you've found the right lender, your challenge is to find the right loan for your specific situation.

We'll briefly consider three types of financing in turn: construction financing, bridge/mini-perm financing, and permanent financing.

- Construction Loans

Typically, the costs of developing your own facility will be covered by a construction loan. This loan may be used to acquire the land and/or construct buildings on land already under your control. Construction loans are typically secured by personal guarantees.

A construction loan usually runs for 24 to 36 months. You should always negotiate an option to renew this loan (via extensions) at least twice. Make sure that you give your-self enough time to build your project, get through the initial period, and develop stable cash flow. Many developers box themselves into a corner by taking out a construction loan for a period that is too short for their needs. Bankers unfamiliar with self-storage compound this problem by granting short-term construction loans.

Typical leverage is around 70 percent of cost. Note that this is a relationship-driven loan often best served by a local bank.

Items typically financed by a construction loan include:

- ~ Land Acquisition
- ~ Soft Costs
- ~ A and D Costs (see above)
- ~ Entitlements to Permit Costs and Fees
- ~ Interest Carry
- ~ Operational Deficits
- ~ Hard Costs
- ~ Start-Up Costs
- ~ Marketing
- ~ Management
- ~ Furniture Fixtures and Equipment
- ~ Office Furniture
- ~ Phones
- ~ Fax machines
- ~ Copiers
- ~ Printers
- ~ Computers
- ~ Golf Cart
- ~ Hall Carts
- ~ On-Site Signage

~ Cost of Construction Insurance
~ Construction Contingency
~ Construction/Lease-up Real Estate Taxes
~ Partnership Legal Fees
~ Developer's Fees
~ Loan Fees

• Bridge Loans/Mini-Perm Loans

Bridge loans are usually expensive, short term loans of three years or less. They are often used to help close a transaction quickly. Bridge loans can also be taken out to pay-off and replace construction loans that fall due before building is completed.

Mini-perm or mini-permanent loans are the preferred choice of self-storage developers seeking short-term loans. A mini-perm loan combines a construction loan with a permanent loan. It starts out as an interest-only loan and at stabilization converts to an amortizing loan. Costs typically financed by a mini-perm loan include:

~ Acquisition and Development (A&D) Costs
~ "A-to-Z" Construction Costs
~ Start-Up Costs

Mini-perm loans are usually 48 to 60 months in length, and are typically full-recourse loans. Strong borrowers may be able to negotiate partial releases as debt service coverage targets are achieved.

• Permanent Loans

The Permanent Loan is often used to pay off construction, mini-perm, or bridge loans. It is typically a five to ten year loan with a 25-year amortization. This loan is often sought from conduit lenders, as it isn't intended to be refinanced in the short term (hence the name "Permanent Loan").

The permanent loan, if non-recourse, can be a great alternative to a sale. Compare for example, high loan-to-value (LTV) financing (advance rate of 75 to 80 percent) versus the sale of a property with a very low basis. If you are facing this type of choice, ask your accountant and legal counsel to review the specific circumstances and make a recommendation.

PREPARING YOUR LOAN APPLICATION

It's important to begin preparing your loan application well in advance. You can choose to do it yourself or pay a professional to put together a good loan package (See Appendix I for a Sample Loan Application).

The quality of your presentation can make a huge difference in the processing of your loan. Make certain that you can answer all the questions a lender might ask, and be prepared to provide supporting documentation. Do your homework well ahead of time. A good self-storage consultant can prepare the loan package for you.

- Loan Request

One of the most critical elements in the loan application process is the initial executive summary or loan request document that you provide to the lender. This document should be very succinct and yet comprehensive enough to cover all of the salient facts of the loan. Know what the lender's approximate loan terms are, and make your request conform to the lender's requirements. If for example, you know the lender will not lend at par (no points) avoid requesting a no-point loan. Before you submit your loan request, understand the lender's underwriting requirements. If you know the advance rate, or loan-to-value is at a maximum of 75 percent, don't try for an 80 percent loan. Save your negotiating power for the most critical elements, such as rates and terms.

The executive summary or loan request should be a "pull out" or stand-alone document so that it may be easily copied. It should be provided in digital and hard copy format.

- Supporting Documentation

Organize all of the supporting information required to document everything in your loan request. Supporting documentation should prove and support everything in your Executive Summary. The information should be indexed and tabbed for easy reference. It should be separate, but include a copy of the executive summary.

Following these guidelines can help you to obtain the best possible financing for your circumstances. Remember that the best loan is the loan that meets your needs. Be prepared, focused, and show the financier that you are both on the same team by responding quickly to questions and requests for documentation.

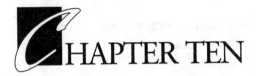

CHAPTER TEN

WHAT'S NEXT FOR SELF-STORAGE?

As we look ahead, it's clear to us that the future looks very bright for self-storage. As our industry continues to grow, we anticipate the strengthening of several trends that are already beginning to take shape within the industry.

The following lists a few of these trends.

- A Growing Need for Self-Storage

The U.S. population is predicted to reach 400 million by 2050. Chances are that we'll continue to be highly mobile and to accumulate stuff. This means that there will be an additional 150 million potential customers looking for somewhere to store their belongings securely.

- State-of-the-Art Facilities

An increasingly sophisticated customer base will force owners of older facilities to make improvements in order to remain competitive. This will result in more trophy properties, offering better layouts, larger offices, flexible unit mixes, and other sought after amenities. We can also expect an acceleration of today's trend towards upscale Main Street locations.

- Cities Demand Mixed Use Facilities

As self-storage facilities move closer to Main Street, many cities will require them to have a retail component in order to increase the amount of sales tax generated and paid to those cities.

- A Broader Range of Products and Services

In addition to increasing the number of customized services for their users, self-storage facilities will move toward becoming mixed use destinations. We'll also begin to see major partnerships formed with businesses that provide complementary products and services. This may include for example, combining storage with a Kinko's to attract business clients or putting a store such as Starbucks or Subway Sandwiches on the ground floor with storage above.

- Customer Service Becomes Job #1

As the customer base widens, a broader range of people will be expecting more from the self-storage experience. These customers will demand excellence and they will quickly take their dollars elsewhere whenever they are disappointed with service levels.

Conversely, when customers are pleased with the service they receive they will return again and again (and even tell their friends). The self-storage facilities that thrive in this competitive arena will be the stores that nurture and retain these loyal customers for life.

In this way, self-storage will become more and more like the hotel business. Tomorrow's owners will respond to competition for customer loyalty with dedicated frequent user programs similar to those used by hotels and airlines.

- The Industry Grows Up

An increasing number of self-storage companies will go public on Wall Street. This will create a demand for sophisticated industry data and better financial reporting that will encourage sophisticated investors to put their money to work in this space.

- Increased Competition

We can expect more building and competition in almost every market, here and over-seas. In some areas, this may lead to overbuilding. Either way, owners will need to work harder and smarter to attract and retain customers.

- More Consolidation/Branding

It's highly likely that we'll see more consolidation as large and mid-sized self-storage companies find ways to merge their operations or acquire their rivals. This will increase the trend toward local, regional and national brands.

- Cashing Out

In the next few years there will be big winners and big losers in the self-storage industry. In many cases, the winners will be distinguished from the losers by:

~ Rational vs. irrational decision making

~ Patience and persistence

• A Few Bumps Ahead

~ The recent run-up in prices almost guarantees that some deals will close at inflated prices. Down the road, these stores may not succeed.
~ In addition, overbuilding will lead to a saturated, fragmented market in many areas creating problems for unsophisticated owners.

• A Steady Increase in Value for Well-Located Self-Storage Facilities

In the years ahead, this ongoing trend will continue, thanks to a variety of factors, including:

~ Low interest rates
~ Increasing popularity and visibility of self-storage as an investment opportunity
~ A continuation of the Wall Street "jitters" that have prompted investors to transfer funds from the stock market to real estate opportunities
~ A large influx of exchange buyers looking to spend their 1031 dollars.
   ○ These individuals will help keep property prices high. They're investors who have sold property and need to buy a similar property in order to defer taxes. Because they have to buy within a certain time period, these forced purchases often drive prices higher.

~ See "A Growing Need for Self-Storage" earlier in this chapter.
~ Still the Best Investment for Those Who Do It Right

Whatever the future has in store, chances are that self-storage will remain a predicable, stable, low-maintenance, high cash-flow investment for those who do it right.

GLOSSARY

ACTUAL NUMBERS (also see Proforma) • In income or other financial statements, actual numbers reflect what is actually occurring or has occurred at the self-storage facility. It's always important to distinguish between proforma (projected numbers) and actual numbers.

BREAK-EVEN OCCUPANCY • The occupancy level at which a self-storage facility's expenses and revenues are equal is referred to as break-even occupancy. A facility's occupancy rate will exceed break-even and show a profit when gross rent exceeds expenses plus debt service. In the industry's early days, the break-even occupancy point for storage was much lower than that of other property types. A typical facility could reach break-even at 55- to 65-percent occupancy. In recent years, higher land and building costs have brought the self-storage break-even point closer to those of retail, industrial, and housing.

CAPITALIZATION RATE • In real estate, the expected annual rate of return on a property is called the capitalization rate or cap rate. (Not to be confused as written with cash-on-cash or internal rate of return, the cap rate is a valuation element.) A cap rate is the number, expressed as a percentage, that is divided into income to indicate value (IRV – Income/Rate = Value). Cap rates can be derived from comparable sales data, but indicate several perspectives—actual, trailing, and stabilized are the most common. A cap rate of 10 for example, suggests that the buyer can expect an annual return of 10 percent.

COMPETITIVE MARKET RADIUS • The area surrounding a self-storage facility is referred to as the competitive market radius. This is the area in which that facility is competing for customers. According to the Self Storage Association, 95 percent of the average facility's tenants either live or work within a three- to five-mile competitive market radius. As the number of facilities increases in a market, the competitive radius tends to decrease so, on average, an area with many competing facilities will have a smaller competitive market radius.

CONVERSION • The process by which an existing structure is re-purposed for use as self-storage space is called a conversion. In this way, for example, old warehouses or manufacturing plants are converted into self-storage facilities by adding a small office and putting up dividing walls to create lockable, private spaces.

DEFERRED MAINTENANCE • The overall impact of postponing or neglecting maintenance and other required periodic repairs is referred to as deferred maintenance. This may save money in the short-term, but usually results in more costly repairs that could have been avoided by regular upkeep and scheduled maintenance.

DUE DILIGENCE (ALSO SEE FEASIBILITY STUDY) • The discovery and verification process of all of the details involved in a real estate transaction before proceeding with that deal is called due diligence.

DEBT SERVICE • Payments made on a loan are the debt service. A facility's profit (or loss) can be calculated by subtracting debt service obligations from net operating income (before debt service).

DEVELOPMENT • Building a facility to your own specifications is called development. The developer is typically the private investor who initiates and supervises this process, including site selection, entitlement, planning, building, financing, management, advertising and lease up.

DIVERSIFICATION • In investing, diversification refers to a technique for reducing the potential for losses. Buying only one stock makes you vulnerable to changes in the value of that stock. If its price plummets, so does your entire investment. Hold ten stocks from ten different sectors in a portfolio instead and, chances are good that they won't all lose value at the same time. Think of diversification as an economic application of the old adage, "Don't put all of your eggs in one basket."

ECONOMIC OCCUPANCY (ALSO SEE PHYSICAL OCCUPANCY) • The actual rents that a facility's storage units generate is referred to as the economic occupancy. It factors in all discounts and incentives applied to the rents.

FEASIBILITY STUDY • Before committing to developing a self-storage facility, you need to conduct a thorough feasibility study. Like due diligence, feasibility studies will help you to decide whether or not you should move forward with your investment plan. The difference is that due diligence studies are conducted before buying, while feasibility studies are undertaken before building begins.

GENERATIONS • To date, we have seen three generations of self-storage facilities:

FIRST GENERATION (1965-1988) • In the early days of self-storage, metal buildings with rows of garage doors were built in industrial parks, or on land that would otherwise have been unused.

SECOND GENERATION (1989-1993) • The second generation of self-storage was characterized by improvements such as better locations, paved driveways, security technology, and Real Estate Investment Trusts.

THIRD GENERATION (1993-present) • Today's state-of-the-art self-storage facilities are very different from their predecessors. Many of these stores, for example, do not even look like self-storage facilities. Other features include high-traffic and high-visibility locations, great signage, zoned temperature and humidity control, and business-oriented customer areas.

GROSS INCOME • The pre-tax figure calculated by subtracting the facility's costs from the total amount of rental and other revenues is its gross income.

LAND BANKING • The practice of acquiring land and holding it for future use is referred to as land banking. The idea is to buy land before expanding urbanization increases its value.

LEASE UP • Also known as absorption, lease up refers to the period of time needed to fill a self-storage facility with renters. A self-storage facility is considered fully rented or leased up at 85- to 90-percent occupancy.

LEVERAGE • The process of creating positive cash flow by using borrowed money is leverage. In real estate, leverage can allow you to control a property worth millions by making relatively small payments on a mortgage or other loan.

LOAN REQUEST • The "Loan Request" document summarizes all the salient facts regarding a particular loan. Prepared for the lender by the loan applicant, this document is one of the most critical elements in the loan application process. The "Loan Request" document must be succinct and yet comprehensive enough to cover all of the loan's salient facts.

MARKET SATURATION • One of the self-storage industry's ongoing debates focuses on over-building or market saturation as it is known in financial circles. This debate is ongoing because we have few yardsticks for determining when a particular market has reached equilibrium in terms of supply and demand.

MEDIAN INCOME • When determining an average income within a specific set or group, the entire range of incomes is arranged in order, with the middle one being designated as the median income. For example, if there were 100 salaries, the median salary would be the wage paid to the employee ranked 50th.

NET OPERATING INCOME (NOI) • Subtracting a facility's expenses from its income will give you the store's net operating income (NOI) before debt service.

PASSIVE INCOME • The income from a passive activity is referred to as its passive income. This includes earnings from a rental property, limited partnership, or other enterprise in which you are not actively involved.

PHYSICAL OCCUPANCY (ALSO SEE ECONOMIC OCCUPANCY) • The actual number of units or square feet rented at a facility, without regard to rental rates, is referred to as its physical occupancy.

PROFORMA NUMBERS • In income or other financial statements, the proforma numbers are projected figures based on an estimate of what could happen. It's important to distinguish between proforma (projected numbers) and the actual figures. Actual numbers reflect what is actually occurring or has occurred at the facility. Be very wary about committing to a deal based on the seller's proforma figures.

REAL ESTATE INVESTMENT TRUSTS (REITS) • A trust that uses the pooled capital of many investors to purchase, develop, and manage income property and/or mortgage loans is called a Real Estate Investment Trust or REIT. REITs are traded on major exchanges just like stocks, and are granted special tax considerations. Real Estate Investment Trusts that specialize in self-storage facilities allow you to invest in a professionally-managed portfolio of self-storage properties.

SECURITIZED DEBT • Securities (bonds) that are actually secured by assets are known as securitized debt. In other words, the loan against a property is actually secured by the real estate (self-storage property). If the borrower does not pay on the loan, the lender can foreclose on the property, thereby reducing the risk associated with the loan.

SITE LAYOUT • A project's ground map is its site layout. In most cases, the owner works with a local architect or civil engineer familiar with self-storage and local zoning regulations to develop a ground map that maximizes the size and shapes of the buildings without violating regulations regarding setbacks, drainage, fire lanes, etc.

SITE SELECTION • The process of choosing the right community or location for your self-storage investment is the site selection process.

STATE OF THE ART • The highest level of development of, for example, self-storage facilities, built at a particular time is referred to as state of the art. For instance, third-generation facilities built today with all of the bells and whistles in terms of security, access technology, and management software, are considered to be state of the art.

APPENDIX A: TOP 100 SELF-STORAGE OPERATORS

#	2004 Ranking	Firm Name	# of Facilities	# of Units	Total Net Rentable Square Footage	Facility Average
1	1	Public Storage, Inc.	1,442	824,484	87,324,000	60,558
2	2	Shurgard Storage Centers, Inc.	616	283,369**	39,000,000	63,312
3	3	Storage USA	482	317,900	33,200,000	68,880
4	4	U-Haul International, Inc.	1,044	377,852**	32,910,418	31,523
5	5	Sovran Self Storage	271	140,000	16,100,000	59,410
6	6	U-Store-It	165	93,172	10,154,533	61,543
7	7	Extra Space Storage	125	78,400	8,165,000	65,320
8	8	Derrel's Mini Storage, Inc.	43	52,148	7,132,467	165,871
9	9	A-American Storage Management Co., Inc	100	64,344	6,600,129	66,001
10	10	Private Mini Storage	80	46,000	5,770,000	72,125
11	11	National Self Storage Management, Inc.	93	48,908	5,359,280	57,627
12	12	Dahn Corporation	85	50,000	5,200,000	61,176
13	13	Storage Inns, Inc.	100	*	5,000,000	50,000
14	14	Morningstar Properties, LLC	58	32,000	4,486,000	77,345
15	15	Pegasus Group	54	36,300	4,320,000	80,000
16	16	Nolan Brothers, Inc./Nolan Brothers of Texas, Inc.	53	33,873	4,115,602	77,653
17	17	SecurCare Self Storage, Inc.	106	35,171	4,095,000	38,632
18	18	TNT Self Storage Management, Inc.	50	63,000	4,012,000	80,240
19	19	Metro Storage LLC	63	33,800	3,900,000	61,905
20	20	Platinum Storage Group	40	34,000	3,625,000	90,625
21	21	Stor-All Systems, Inc.	43	24,563	3,237,395	75,288
22	22	Brundage Management, Inc.	45	26,763	3,100,000	68,889
23	23	Liberty Investment Properties, Inc.	41	27,000	3,000,000	73,171
24	24	Republic Storage of Idaho	14	13,962	2,852,081	203,720
25	25	Kevin Howard Real Estate	53	23,141	2,752,426	51,933
26	26	BACO Realty Corporation	37	27,827	2,695,500	72,851
27	27	Chesapeake Resources, Inc.	35	26,380	2,607,958	74,513
28	28	Executive Self Storage Associates, Inc.	51	26,000	2,600,000	50,980
28	28	Self Storage Management Company	27	17,967	2,600,000	96,296
29	29	StorageMart	39	23,446	2,571,575	65,938
30	30	LAACO, Ltd.	36	24,624	2,564,241	71,229
31	31	Landvest Corporation	51	21,054	2,522,632	49,463
32	32	Accountable Mangement & Realty, Inc.	43	21,892	2,505,611	58,270
33	33	AAAAA Rent A Space	17	20,000	2,500,000	147,059
34	34	Westport Properties, Inc./US Storage Centers	35	24,784	2,418,425	69,098
35	35	Arizona Mini Storage Management Company	40	20,186	2,161,053	54,026
36	36	Caster Properties, Inc.	30	21,301	2,152,000	71,733
37	37	Devon Self-Storage	22	15,161	2,119,293	96,332
38	38	Urban Self Storage, Inc.	31	19,538	2,089,000	67,387
39	39	Universal Management Company	30	16,246	2,041,924	68,064
40	40	BMS Management Company	18	20,000	2,000,000	111,111
41	41	Mini-Management Services	18	15,010	1,989,473	110,526
42	42	Pogoda Companies	40	15,000	1,975,000	49,375
43	43	Shader Brothers Corp./Personal Mini Storage Management	30	16,507	1,971,523	65,717
44	44	America West Management	32	17,239	1,863,768	58,243
45	45	OB Companies	31	15,185	1,803,202	58,168
46	46	The Nicholson Companies/AAAA Self Storage Management Group	32	*	1,752,652	54,770
47	47	StorageWorld, LP	26	15,129	1,750,800	67,338
48	48	The Jenkins Organization, Inc.	20	14,000	1,700,000	85,000
49	49	Hendry Investments, Inc.	21	15,231	1,682,150	80,102
50	50	Lock Up Storage Centers	25	17,951	1,659,325	66,373

* Information Not Provided   ** Does not include units owned internationally

Note: The top operator's list is based on those companies that provided information to the Mini-Storage Messenger. It should be noted that there are some large operators that do not report ownership data.

SOURCE: *2005 Self-Storage Almanac*

#	2004 Ranking	Firm Name	# of Facilities	# of Units	Total Net Rentable Square Footage	Facility Average
51	51	BPI Capital Management, Inc.	24	13,359	1,630,900	67,954
52	52	Price Self Storage	9	14,350	1,600,000	177,778
53	52	Investment Development Corporation	27	15,600	1,600,000	59,259
54	53	Cornerstone Development Corporation	21	10,316	1,473,043	70,145
55	54	Storage Assets, LLC/ Lackland Self Storage	17	14,306	1,445,789	85,046
56	55	Absolute Storage Management, Inc.	20	10,700	1,400,000	70,000
57	56	Southern Self Storage	20	12,230**	1,375,338	68,767
58	57	Metro Mini Storage	15	7,850	1,375,000	91,667
59	58	The William Warren Group	21	13,771	1,373,158	65,388
60	59	All Seasons Storage Trust	25	10,842	1,336,465	53,459
61	60	SKS Management, LLC	14	12,993	1,322,815	94,487
62	61	Riteplace Management, Inc.	20	9,808	1,322,685	66,134
63	62	Management Enterprises, Inc/All Aboard Mini Storage	23	12,081	1,315,837	57,210
64	63	Brookwood Properties, LLC	14	9,052	1,227,230	87,659
65	64	Gainer Management Associates, Inc.	19	7,200	1,215,000	63,947
66	65	Noah's Ark Development	18	11,259	1,184,760	65,820
67	66	Cutting Edge Self Storage Management & Consulting, Inc.	17	7,567	1,176,272	69,192
68	67	Sterling Management & Consulting, Inc.	16	9,872	1,166,324	72,895
69	68	Mirabito, Mooney & Associates	12	10,134	1,145,013	95,418
70	69	American Self Storage Corporation	15	10,458	1,112,435	74,162
71	70	Synergy Storage Group	17	11,783	1,112,000	65,412
72	71	U.S. Storage Depot, LLC	8	6,539	1,100,892	137,612
73	72	Investment Real Estate Management, LLC	28	9,206	1,097,206	39,186
74	73	Stor-All	16	8,291	1,086,122	67,883
75	74	American Storage	28	9,249	1,073,467	38,338
76	75	Hide-Away Storage, LLC	12	9,000	1,050,000	87,500
77	76	Revest Management Services, Inc.	15	7,700	1,040,000	69,333
78	77	Paul Darden Company	17	*	1,022,000	60,118
79	78	Capital Management and Realty	15	10,674	1,016,558	67,771
80	79	Storage Deluxe	12	17,000	1,000,000	83,333
81	80	American Self Storage	13	14,869	994,668	76,513
82	81	Professional Self Storage Management, LLC	21	8,710	992,000	47,238
83	82	Storage Investment Mangement, Inc.	23	9,323	990,338	43,058
84	83	Liberty Self-Stor	20	7,768	990,130	49,507
85	84	Watson & Taylor & Management Company, Inc.	16	6,301	987,634	61,727
86	85	Strategic Property Management, Inc.	15	8,191	967,355	64,490
87	86	Incorporated Investments, Inc.	15	7,869	963,694	64,246
88	87	Sentry Self Storage Management	14	8,900	955,000	68,214
89	88	Automated Properties Management, Ltd.	17	9,842	951,737	55,985
90	89	Polo Properties, LLC	14	10,000	935,000	66,786
91	90	Rearden Investments	14	8,717	924,000	66,000
92	91	The Freeman Mangement Group	16	7,282	921,049	57,566
93	92	Advance Management	9	7,114	899,352	99,928
94	93	Your Extra Attic, Inc.	16	6,399	879,980	54,999
95	94	Long Property Management	9	6,700	855,600	95,067
96	95	Attic Storage	12	5,210	848,643	70,720
97	96	Access Management Company	13	10,060	832,252	64,019
98	97	Stockade Storage	12	6,676	814,060	67,838
99	98	C.N. Lyons Development Company	10	9,396	802,467	80,247
100	99	Stor-N-Lock Companies	14	7,568	780,393	55,742
101	100	Anchor Investment Corporation of Florida	11	6,400	767,000	69,727
TOTAL			6,895	3,432,957	415,557,097	72,662

* Information Not Provided   ** Does not include units owned internationally

Note: The top operator's list is based on those companies that provided information to the Mini-Storage Messenger. It should be noted that there are some large operators that do not report ownership data.

SOURCE: *2005 Self-Storage Almanac*

APPENDIX B: SAMPLE TARGET PROPERTY LIST

TARGET PROPERTY LIST

	Facility Name	Street Address	Business Phone	Lot Size	Rent Sq/Ft	Units	Asking Price	Offer Price	Status
1									
2									
3									
4									
5									
6									
7									
8									
9									
10									
11									
12									
13									
14									
15									
16									
17									
18									
19									
20									
21									
22									
23									
24									
25									

APPENDIX C: SELF-STORAGE INSTITUTIONAL GRADE CRITRIA

Land Size:	Two to five acres
Building Size:	50,000 net rentable square feet
Topography:	Mostly level with adequate drainage
Environmental:	Typical to R.E.I.T. standards Residential deed restrictions acceptable Will consider impaired but insurable sites
Demographics:	One-mile population = 25,000 + Three-mile population = 75,000 + Five-mile population = 125,000 +
Population Growth:	Greater than two percent per annum
Median Household Income:	$45,000 or greater
Traffic Counts:	Greater than 20,000 cars per day, or top two percent of market
Access:	Direct from traffic count criteria street. Consider no more than three turns to entry
Zoning:	Authorized use with letter from municipality to verify
Barrier to Entry:	High for self-storage competitors by virtue of economics or zoning
Competitive Evaluation:	Competitors acceptable if stabilized occupancy of 87 percent has been reached
Marketing:	One-third-page ad in *Yellow Pages*
Replacement Cost:	Not to Exceed 1.2x
Cap Rate Range:	8.0 percent to 10 percent

APPENDIX D: SAMPLE SINGLE FACILITY ONE-YEAR PROFIT & LOSS STATEMENT (STABLIZIED FACILITY)

Rentable Square Feet	50,000	
Price Per SQ/FT	$1.00	
Income	Amount	% Total Income
Gross Rents At 100% Occupancy	600,000.00	
Less Vacancy At 10%	60,000.00	
Subtotal Gross Rents	540,000.00	95%
Miscellaneous Products & Services	27,000.00	5%
Total Income	567,000.00	100%
Expenses	Amount	% Gross Income
Salaries & Related Items	45,360	8.00%
Management Fees	34,020	6.00%
Property Taxes	51,030	9.00%
Advertising - *Yellow Pages*	17,010	3.00%
Repairs & Maintenance	5,670	1.00%
Utilities - Phone, Water, Electricity, Gas	11,340	2.00%
Office Supplies, Postage, Printing	2,835	0.50%
Professional Fees	2,835	0.50%
Insurance	11,340	2.00%
Marketing & Promotion	2,835	0.50%
Miscellaneous	2,835	0.50%
Total Expenses	187,110	33%
Total Expense As A Percent of Income		33%
Total Expense Per Rentable SQ/FT		3.74
Net Operating Income (Before Debt Service)	379,890	
Less Debt Service		
Net Profit/Cash Remaining For Distribution		

Appendix E: Sample Feasibility Checklist

FEASIBILITY ITEMS	STATUS
Self-Storage Industry Data	
Area, Location, and Competition Map	
Project Description	
Property Photographs	
Community Data	
Municipality Data	
Flood Map	
Macro and Micro Site Analysis	
Square Feet Of Storage Per Capita	
Market Demand Analysis	
Definition and Comment On Primary Market	
Definition and Comment On Secondary Market	
Competitive Analysis - Primary Market	
Competitive Analysis - Secondary Market	
Proposed Unit Mix	
Proposed Rental Rates	
Absorption Analysis	
Exit Strategy	
Store Operations Plan	
Insurance Quote	
Quote for *Yellow Pages*	
Construction Cost Estimates	
5 To 7 Year Month-By-Month Budgets	
Investment Return Analysis	
Conclusion and Recommendations	

Appendix F: Sample Facility Walk-Through Report

	GENERAL FACILITY INFORMATION
Facility Name	
Business Address	
Phone Number	
Parcel Number	
Zoning	
Lot Size	
Rentable Sq/Ft	
Total Units	
Construction Type	

	FEATURES & BENEFITS
DRIVE UP	
Visibility	
Traffic Count	
HighwayAccess	
Curb Appeal	
Paved Driveways	
Special Features	
RETAIL OPERATION	
Retail Store (Y/N)	
Locks, Boxes, And Supplies	
PO Boxes	
Move-In Truck	
Highly Educated And Friendly Staff	
SECURITY	
Resident Manager	
Perimeter Fencing	
Electronic Gates	
Keypad Entry/Exit	
Video Surveillance	
Sign-In Sheet	
Individual Door Alarms	
Well Lighted Halls	
Lights In Each Unit	
Fire Sprinklers	
Pest Control	
Break-Ins?	

CONVENIENCE	
External Drive-Up Units	
Internal Drive-Up Units	
Multistory	
Elevators	
Lifts	
Hallway Units	
Wide Aisles	
Wide Doors	
Lighting	
Music Playing In Hallways	
Climate Control	
Carts & Dollies	
Access Hours	
Automatic Payment	
Credit Cards	
Electronic Check In / Kiosks	
Handicap Access	
TECHNOLOGY	
Management Software	
Computerized Accounting	
Computer Software Programs	
MARKETING	
Yellow Pages	
Web Site	
Brochures	
Apartment Program	
Business Program	
New Tenant Survey	
On-Line Payment	
Referral Program	
Move-In Truck	
Banners	
Storage Hints	
Business Cards	
Signage	

Appendix G: Ten Items to Include In Your Purchase and Sale Agreement

1. Add a Non-Compete Clause – Five Years / Five Miles

When selling a business, most sellers are accustomed to a non-compete clause. Start with these parameters (five years/five miles) and you can soften either term to help get the deal done. An alternative could be to get a first right of refusal on the sale of any project the developer builds within a five-mile radius.

2. Have Your Due Diligence Commence Upon Receipt from the Seller of All Due Diligence Materials

Sellers can drag their feet in getting you the documents you need to analyze their property effectively, and the clock is running if you have not adequately protected yourself with a clause similar to this. An alternative approach could be to specify a number of days within which you are to receive the documents. If these documents are not delivered, add an additional day to the inspection period for each additional day that the due diligence materials are not delivered.

3. Make Sure to Get Copies of All Previously Conducted Reports

Receiving copies of previously conducted reports including surveys, title policies, appraisals, Phase 1 & 2 reports, and soils and engineering studies can short circuit the due diligence process and cut to the chase. Moreover, money can oftentimes be saved by going back to earlier providers of due diligence materials. Note that most professionals have certain reliance language and if you ever have a claim, you will want the reports issued to you, not the seller.

4. Only Count Business Days vs. Calendar Days

This is our favorite technique to getting more free time.

5. Make Any and All Deposits OK to Place Within Three Days of the Date Due

Sometimes it is not practical or even possible to get earnest money to the seller on the day of the deadline. This clause allows for a little breathing room. It is not meant to buy more time, only to enable you to meet deadlines in rare circumstances where an extra day or two are needed. This is very helpful when dealing across country and money needs to be wired or sent via courier.

6. Make Sure Representations and Warranties Survive the Close of Escrow

Check with your attorney—some information may need to be referred to as "post close" in order to be deemed accurate if you are relying on it. This may be the only recourse you have if the seller was trying to defraud you.

7. Final Accounting

Make sure the seller provides close-out accounting from date of the last financial statement through the time period that all bills are paid. This is particularly helpful when refinancing or if you are "flipping" the property soon after close. This tip alone can be worth many times the cost of this book, and it is a little known, but often revered contract clause.

8. Make an Accounts Payable Schedule Part of the Due Diligence Materials

Most self-storage transactions are underwritten on a cash basis. If the seller is holding back payables, they could certify the income and expenses on a cash basis to be true and accurate; however, if, for example, there are $15,000 in unpaid bills that the seller is holding until after the close of escrow, you can do the math to calculate the error.

9. Be Sure to Pull ZIP Code and Marketing Reports from the Main Computer

Where do the customers come from? Just before this writing, a property was acquired in a market where the seller is developing another store, and the new store was exculpated from the non-complete clause. An analysis was done of the existing customer base and it was determined that a large percentage of existing tenants came from the ZIP code of the new store and the risk was properly analyzed.

10. Make Extensions Available At a Price to Extend the Close, With Hard Earnest Money

In this world, the unpredictable can be the driving force that delays the legitimate close of a deal. Anyone who has lived through a natural disaster like a major storm, hurricane, or an earthquake knows how disruptive the closing of a bank, the absence of electricity and phones, or damage to the buyer's office can be. While *force majeure* clauses mitigate this risk relative to natural disasters, every once in a while, a third party such as a lender, appraiser, or consultant can cause the deal to get off track and you may need more time. Imagine if the seller has a better offer pending. A clause such as this may save the day.

There are many other clauses the professional negotiator may want to have in your purchase and sale contract. These ideas are only meant to get you and your legal counsel thinking about a few ideas that may be helpful in completing a successful self-storage transaction.

By all means seek legal counsel! I would never go it alone, even after nearly $1 billion dollars in transactions.

APPENDIX H: SAMPLE DUE DILIGENCE CHECKLIST

DUE DILIGENCE ITEMS	STATUS
Market Analysis	
Review Competition	
Municipality Review	
Management Review	
Break-In and Crime Reports	
Verbal Estoppels	
Deferred Maintenance Inspection	
Review Plans	
Title Report	
Appraisal	
Property Tax Analysis	
Environmental Report	
Property Condition Report	
Survey	
Zoning Report	
Seismic Report	
Loan Information	
Conduct Audit	
Impact Of Purchase On Property Taxes	
Ad Assesment for *Yellow Pages*	
Insurance Coverage Analysis	

APPENDIX I: SAMPLE UNIFORM LOAN APPLICATION

This application is designed to be completed by the applicant(s) with the lender's assistance. Applicants should complete this form as "Borrower" or "Co-Borrower", as applicable. Co-Borrower information must also be provided (and the appropriate box checked) when the income or assets of a person other than the "Borrower" (including the Borrower's spouse) will be used as a basis for loan qualification or the income or assets of the Borrower's spouse will not be used as a basis for loan qualification, but his or her liabilities must be considered because the Borrower resides in a community property state, the security property is located in a community property state, or the Borrower is relying on other property located in a community property state as a basis for repayment of the loan.

Mortgage Applied for:				Agency Case Number		Lender Case Number	
Amount	Interest Rate %	No. of Months	Amortization Type: Other (explain): ARM (type):	Fixed Rate GPM			

II. PROPERTY INFORMATION AND PURPOSE OF LOAN

Subject Property Address (street, city, state, zip)	No. of Units
Legal Description of Subject Property (attach description if necessary)	Year Built

Purpose of Loan: Purchase Construction Other (explain): Refinance Construction-Permanent	Property will be: Investment

Complete this line if Construction or Construction-permanent loan.

Year Lot Acquired	Original Cost $	Amount Existing Liens $	(a) Present Value of Lot $	(b) Cost of Improvements $	Total (a+b) $

Complete this line if this is a refinance loan.

Year Acquired	Original Cost $	Amount Existing Liens $	Purpose of Refinance		
			Describe Improvements Made to be made Cost $		

Title will be held in what Name(s)
Source of down payment, settlement charges and/or subordinate financing

Manner in which Title will be held

Estate will be held in:
□ Fee Simple
□ Leasehold (show expiration date)

III. BORROWER INFORMATION

Borrower	**Co-Borrower**
Borrower's Name (include Jr. or Sr. if applicable)	Co-Borrower's Name (include Jr. or Sr. if applicable)
Social Security Number	Driver's License (Passport, Alien I.D.)	Social Security Number	Driver's License (Passport, Alien I.D.)
Date of Birth (mm/dd/yy)	Home Phone (incl. area code)	Years of School	Date of Birth (mm/dd/yy)	Home Phone (incl. area code)	Years of School
Married Separated Unmarried (single, divorced, widowed)	Dependents (not listed by Co-Borrower) No. Ages	Married Separated Unmarried (single, divorced, widowed)	Dependents (not listed by Borrower) No. Ages
Present Address (street, city, state, zip) Own Rent No. Yrs.	Present Address (street, city, state, zip) Own Rent No. Yrs.

If residing at present address for less than two years, complete the following:

Former Address (street, city, state, zip) Own Rent No. Yrs.	Former Address (street, city, state, zip) Own Rent No. Yrs.
Former Address (street, city, state, zip) Own Rent No. Yrs.	Former Address (street, city, state, zip) Own Rent No. Yrs.

IV. EMPLOYMENT INFORMATION

Borrower			**Co-Borrower**		
Name and Address of Employer	Self Employed	Yrs. on this job	Name and Address of Employer	Self Employed	Yrs. on this job
		Yrs. Employed in this line of work/profession			Yrs. Employed in this line of work/profession
Position/Title/Type of Business	Business Phone (incl. Area code)		Position/Title/Type of Business	Business Phone (incl. Area code)	

If employed in current position for less than two years or if currently employed in more than one position complete the following:

Name and Address of Employer	Self Employed	Dates (from-to)	Name and Address of Employer	Self Employed	Dates (from-to)
		Monthly Income $			Monthly Income $
Position/Title/Type of Business	Business Phone (incl. Area code)		Position/Title/Type of Business	Business Phone (incl. Area code)	
Name and Address of Employer	Self Employed	Dates (from-to)	Name and Address of Employer	Self Employed	Dates (from-to)
		Monthly Income $			Monthly Income $
Position/Title/Type of Business	Business Phone (incl. Area code)		Position/Title/Type of Business	Business Phone (incl. Area code)	

CONTINUED

V. MONTHLY INCOME AND COMBINED HOUSING EXPENSE INFORMATION

Gross Monthly Income	Borrower	Co-Borrower	Total	Combined Monthly Housing Expense	Present	Proposed
Base Empl. Income*	$	$	$	Rent	$	$
Overtime	$	$	$	First Mortgage (P&I)	$	$
Bonuses	$	$	$	Other Financing (P&I)	$	$
Commissions	$	$	$	Hazard Insurance	$	$
Dividends/Interest	$	$	$	Real Estate Taxes	$	$
Net Rental Income	$	$	$	Mortgage Insurance	$	$
Other (before completing, see the notice in "describe other income" below	$	$	$	Homeowner Assn. Dues	$	$
				Other	$	$
Total	S	S	S	Total	S	S

*Self Employed Borrower(s) may be required to provide additional documentation such as tax returns and financial statements.

Describe Other Income

Notice: Alimony, child support, or separate maintenance income need not be revealed if the Borrower (B) or Co-Borrower (C) does not choose to have it considered for repaying this loan.

B/C		Monthly Amount
		$
		$
		$

VI. ASSETS AND LIABILITIES

This statement and any applicable supporting schedules may be completed jointly by both married and unmarried Co-borrowers if their assets and liabilities are sufficiently joined so that the Statement can be meaningfully and fairly presented on a combined basis; otherwise separate Statements and Schedules are required. If the Co-Borrower section was completed about a spouse, this Statement and supporting schedules must be completed about that spouse also.
Completed   Jointly   Not Jointly

ASSETS Description	Cash or Market Value	Liabilities and Pledged Assets. List the creditor's name, address and account number for all outstanding debts, including automobile loans, revolving charge accounts, real estate loans, alimony, child support, stock pledges, etc. Use continuation sheet, if necessary. Indicate by (*) those liabilities which will be satisfied upon sale of real estate owned or upon refinancing of the subject property.			
Cash deposit toward purchase held by:	$				
List checking and savings accounts below		**LIABILITIES**	Monthly Payment & Mos. Left to pay	Unpaid Balance	Account No.
Name and address of Bank, S&L, or Credit Union		Name and address of Company	$ Payment/Mos.	$	
Acct. No.	$				
Name and address of Bank, S&L, or Credit Union		Name and address of Company	$ Payment/Mos.	$	
Acct. No.	$				
Name and address of Bank, S&L, or Credit Union		Name and address of Company	$ Payment/Mos.	$	
Acct. No.	$				
Name and address of Bank, S&L, or Credit Union		Name and address of Company	$ Payment/Mos.	$	
Acct. No.	$				
Stocks & Bonds (Company name/number & description)	$	Name and address of Company	$ Payment/Mos.	$	
Life insurance net cash value Face amount:	$	Name and address of Company	$ Payment/Mos.	$	
Subtotal Liquid Assets	$				
Real Estate owned (enter market value from schedule of real estate owned)	$	Name and address of Company	$ Payment/Mos.	$	
Vested interest in retirement fund	$				
Net worth of business(es) owned (attach financial statement)	$	Name and address of Company	$ Payment/Mos.	$	
Automobiles owned (make and year)	$				
Other Assets (itemize)	$	Alimony/Child Support/Separate Maintenance Payments Owed to:	$		
		Total Monthly Payments	$		
a. Total Assets	$	Net Worth (a - b) $		**b. Total Liabilities**	$

VI. ASSETS AND LIABILITIES (Con't.)

Schedule of Real Estate Owned (if additional properties are owned, use continuation sheet)

Property Address (enter S = Sold, PS = Pending Sale, or is it rental being held for income)	Type of Property	Present Market Value	Amount of Mortgage & Liens	Gross Rental Income	Mortgage Payments	Insurance, Maintenance, Taxes & Misc.	Net Rental Income
		$	$	$	$	$	$
		$	$	$	$	$	$
		$	$	$	$	$	$
TOTALS		$	$	$	$	$	$

List any additional names under which credit has previously been received and indicate appropriate creditor names(s) and account number(s):

Alternative Name	Creditor Name	Account Number

VII. DETAILS OF TRANSACTION		VIII. DECLARATIONS				
A. Purchase price		If you answer "Yes" to any questions A through I, please use continuation sheet for explanation.	Borrower Yes No		Co-Borrower Yes No	
B. Alterations, improvements, repairs		A. Are there any outstanding judgements against you?				
C. Land (if acquired separately)		B. Have you declared bankruptcy within the past 7 years?				
D. Refinance (incl. In debts to be paid off)		C. Have you had property foreclosed upon or given title or deed in lieu thereof in the last 7 years?				
E. Estimated prepaid items		D. Are you a party to a lawsuit?				
F. Estimated closing costs		E. Have you directly or indirectly been obligated on any loan, which resulted in foreclosure, transfer of title in lieu of foreclosure, or judgement? (This would include such loans as home mortgage loans, SBA loans, home improvement loans, educational loans, manufactured (mobile) home loans, any mortgage, financial obligation, bond, or loan guarantee. If "Yes", provide details, including date, name and address of Lender, FHA or VA case number, if any, and reasons for the action.)				
G. PMI, MIP, Funding Fee paid in cash		F. Are you presently delinquent or in default on any Federal debt or any other loan, mortgage, financial obligation, bond, or loan guarantee? If "Yes", give details as described in the preceding question.				
H. Discount (if Borrower will pay)		G. Are you obligate to pay alimony, child support or separate maintenance?				
I. Total costs (add items A through H)		H. Is any part of the down payment borrowed?				
J. Subordinate financing		I. Are you a co-maker or endorser on a note?				
K. Borrower's closing costs paid by Seller		J. Are you a U.S. citizen?				
L. Other Credits (explain)		K. Are you a permanent resident alien?				
M. Loan amount (exclude PMI, MIP, Funding Fee financed)		L. Do you intend to occupy the property as your primary residence? If "Yes", complete question below.				
N. PMI, MIF, Funding Fee financed		M. Have you had an ownership interest in a property in the last 3 years? (1) What type of property did you own - Principal Residence (PR), Second Home (SH), or Investment Property (IP)? (2) How did you hold title to the home - solely by yourself (S), jointly with your spouse (SP) or jointly with another person (O)?				
O. Loan amount (add M & N)						
P. Cash to or from borrower (Subtract J, K, L and O from I)						

IX. ACKNOWLEDGEMENT AND AGREEMENT

Each of the undersigned specifically represents to Lender and to Lender's actual or potential agents, brokers, processors, attorneys, insurers, servicers, successors and assigns and agrees and acknowledges that: (1) the information provided in this application is true and correct as of the date set forth opposite my signature and that any intentional or negligent misrepresentation of this information contained in this application may result in civil liability, including monetary damages, to any person who may suffer any loss due to reliance upon any misrepresentation that I have made on this application, and/or in criminal penalties including, but not limited to, fine or imprisonment or both under the provisions of Title 18, United States Code, Sec. 1001, et. Seq.; (2) the loan requested pursuant to this application (the "Loan") will be secured by a mortgage or deed of trust on the property described herein; (3) the property will not be used for any illegal or prohibited purpose or use; (4) all statements made in this application are made for the purpose of obtaining a mortgage loan; (5) the property will be occupied as indicated herein; (6) any owner or servicer of the Loan may verify or re-verify any information contained in the application from any source named in this application, and Lender, its successors or assigns may retain the original and/or an electronic record of this application, even if the Loan is not approved; (7) the Lender and its agents, brokers, insurers, servicers, successors and assigns may continuously rely on the information contained in the application, and I am obligated to amend and/or supplement the information provided in the application if any of the material facts that I have represented herein should change prior to closing of the Loan; (8) in the event my payments on the Loan become delinquent, the owner or servicer of the Loan may, in addition to any other rights and remedies that it may have relating to such delinquency, report my name and account information to one or more consumer credit reporting agencies; (9) ownership of the Loan and/or administration of the Loan account may be transferred with such notice as may be required by law; (10) neither Lender nor its agents, brokers, insurers, servicers, successors or assigns has made any representation or warranty, express or implied, to me regarding the property or the condition or value of the property; and (11) my transmission of this application as an "electronic record" containing my "electronic signature," as those terms are defined in applicable federal and/or state laws (excluding audio and video recordings), or my facsimile transmission of this application containing a facsimile of my signature, shall be as effective, enforceable and valid as if a paper version of this application were delivered containing my original written signature.

Borrower's Signature	Date	Co-Borrower's Signature	Date

LOAN APPLICATION CONTINUATION SHEET

| Use this continuation sheet if you need more space to complete the Residential Loan Application. Mark "B" for Borrower or "C" for Co-Borrower. | Borrower: | Agency Case Number: |
| | Co-Borrower: | Lender Case Number: |

SAMPLE

I/We fully understand that it is a Federal crime punishable by fine or imprisonment, or both, to knowingly make any false statements concerning any of the above facts as applicable under the provisions of Title 18, United States Code, Section 1001, et.seq.

| Borrower's Signature: | Date: | Co-Borrower's Signature: | Date: |

INDEX